I0488159

New Hamburg Ontario Book 1 in Colour Photos, Saving Our History One Photo at a Time

Photography
by Barbara Raué
2014

Series Name:
Cruising Ontario

Book 58: New Hamburg Book 1

Cover photo: 99 Byron Street

Series Name: Cruising Ontario
Saving Our History One Photo at a Time

Photos in full colour
Check the Appendixes in the back of each book for
descriptions of architectural terms and building styles

Other Books by Barbara Raue

Coins of Gold

Arrows, Indians and Love

The Life and Times of Barbara
Volume 1: Inventions That Have Enhanced My Life
Volume 2: Entertainment That I Have Enjoyed
Volume 3: East Coast Trips
Volume 4: Olympics Have Always Intrigued Me
Volume 5: Wonders of the World
Volume 6: Caribbean Cruises We Have Enjoyed
Volume 7: Animals
Volume 8: Storms and Other Major Disasters in My Lifetime
Volume 9: Wars, Terrorist Attacks and Major Disasters

The Cromwell Family Book

New Hamburg

New Hamburg was established in the early 1830s by William Scott. In 1834, cholera killed many of the original settlers of New Hamburg. A grist-mill built by Josiah Cushman about 1834 formed the nucleus around which a small community of Amish Mennonites and recent German immigrants developed. More German and Scottish settlers arrived in the late 1830s and early 1840s. The Grand Trunk railway arrived in the 1850s and the village became an important centre for milling and the production of farm machinery.

New Hamburg is located in the rural township of Wilmot in the Regional Municipality of Waterloo. It is bordered by Baden to the east and is within easy driving distance of the cities of Kitchener, Waterloo and Stratford.

The Nith River winds through town and flows through the downtown core, which is home to a 50-foot waterwheel built in 1990, the largest operating water wheel in North America; a symbol of the importance of the Nith River, and of the water-powered mills which were the first industries in pioneer New Hamburg.

Table of Contents

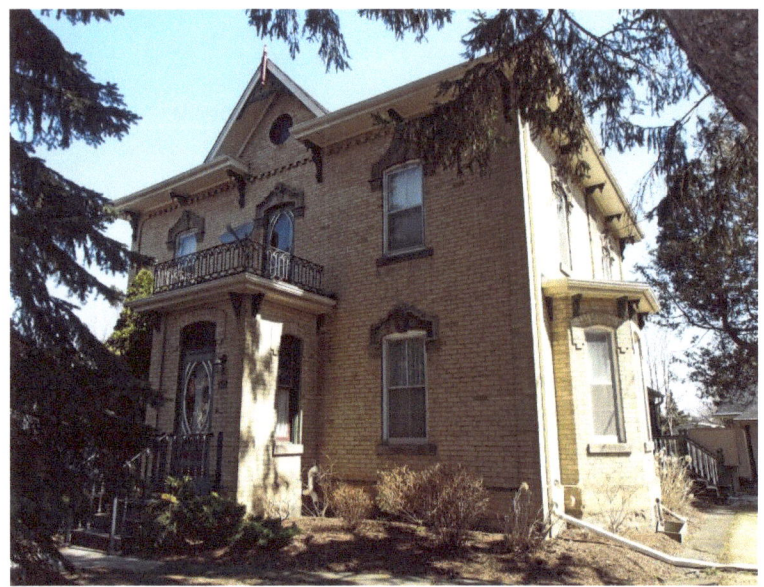

349 Peel Street – Italianate, single cornice brackets, ornate window voussoirs, balcony on second floor, finial on gable

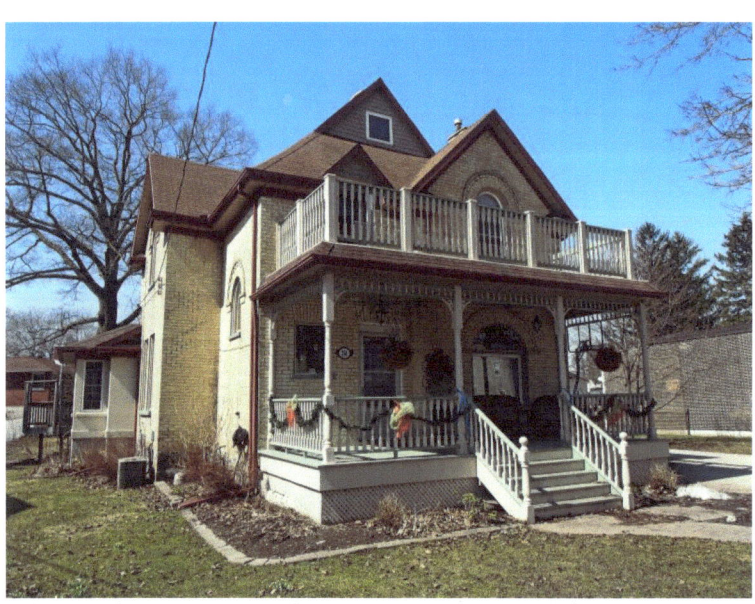

334 Peel Street – Gothic Revival, second floor balcony

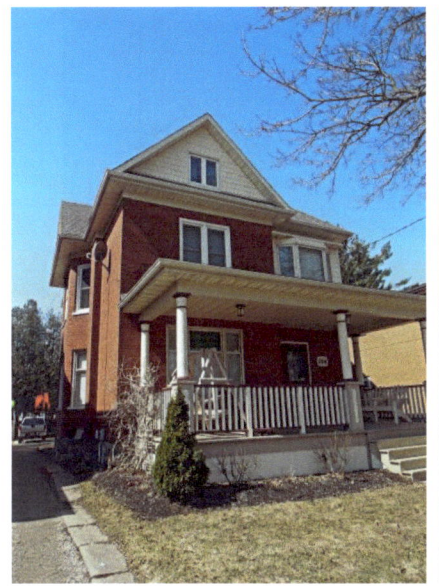
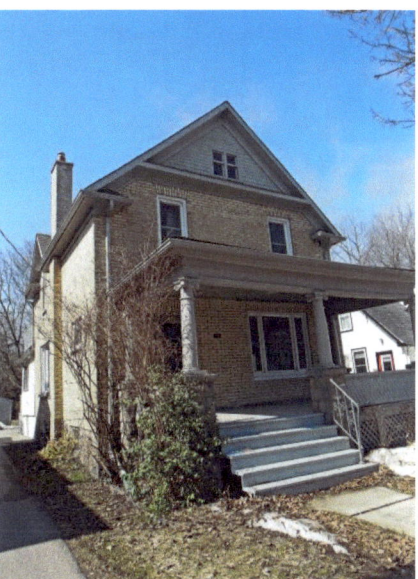

304 Peel Street   250 Peel Street

Edwardian

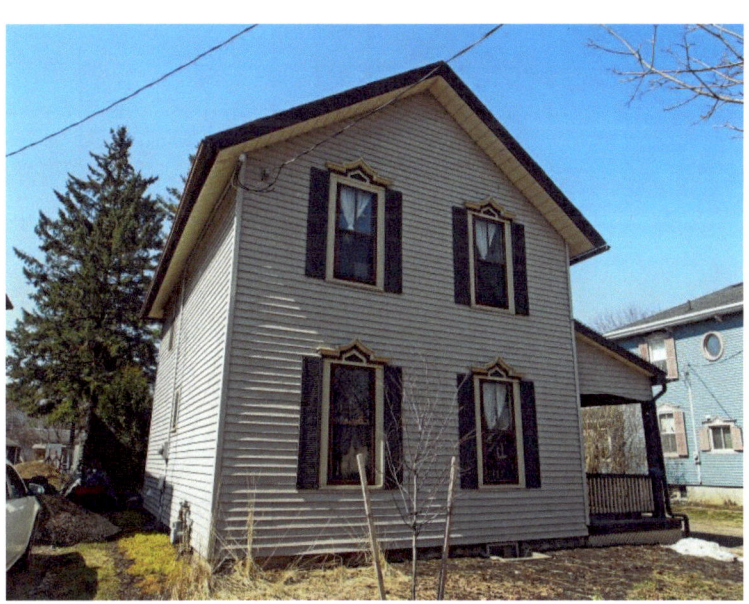

Gothic Revival – decorative window hoods

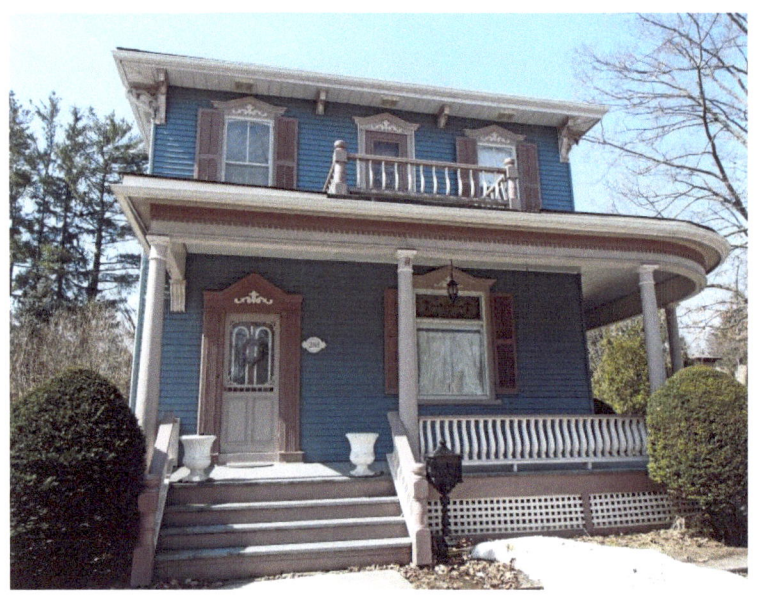

288 Peel Street – Italianate, single cornice brackets, wraparound verandah, balcony on second floor

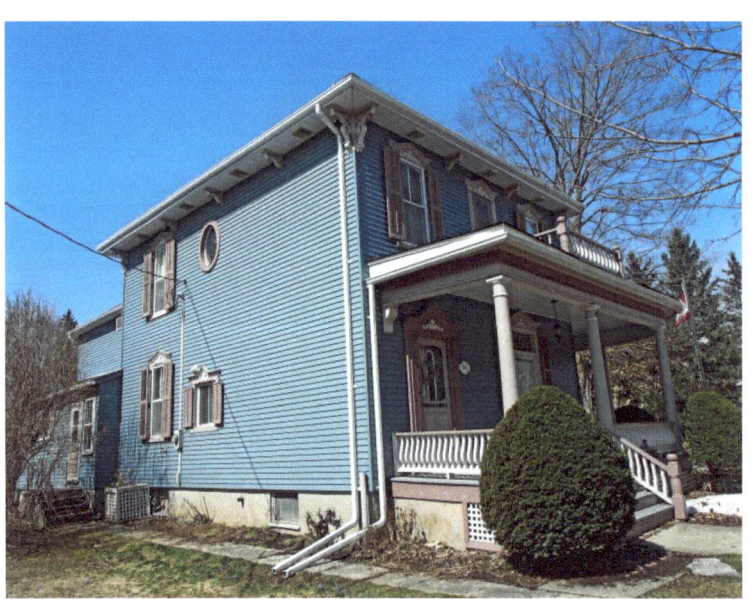

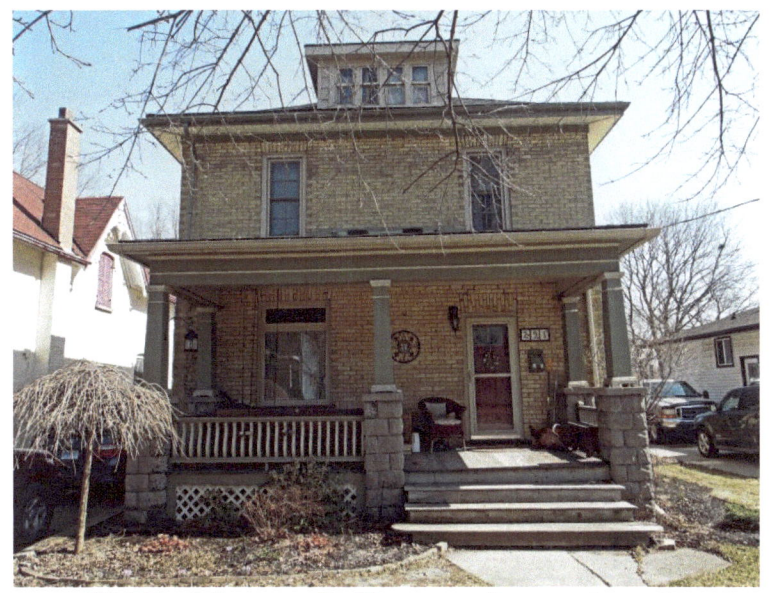

291 Peel Street – Italianate – dormer in attic

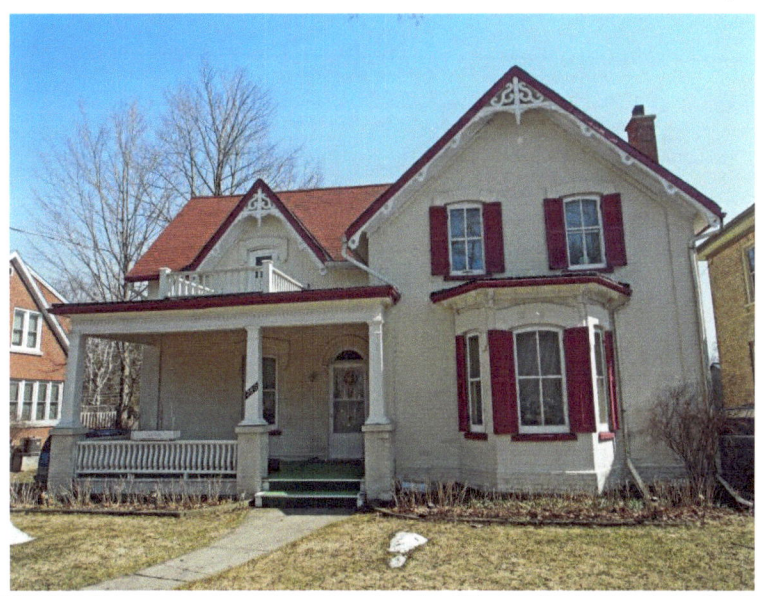

285 Peel Street – Gothic Revival – Vergeboard trim, finial

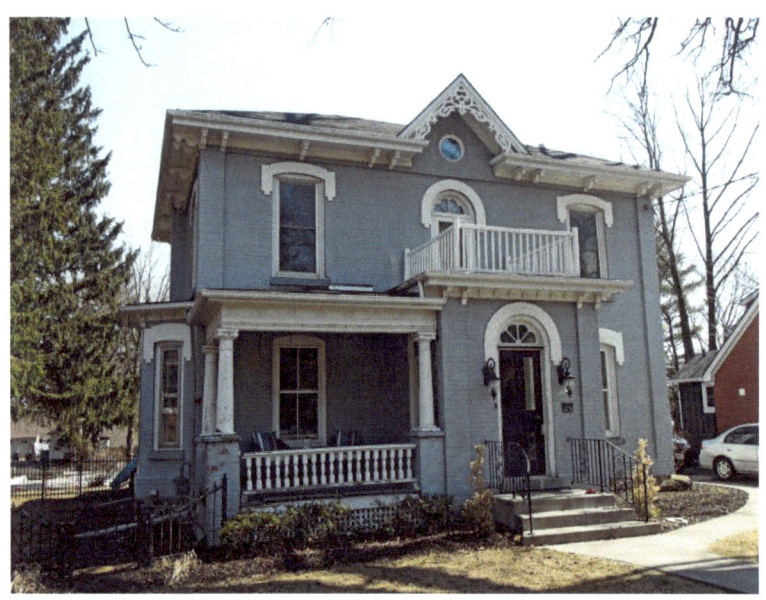

273 Peel Street – Italianate, cornice brackets,
Vergeboard trim, balcony second floor, bay window on side

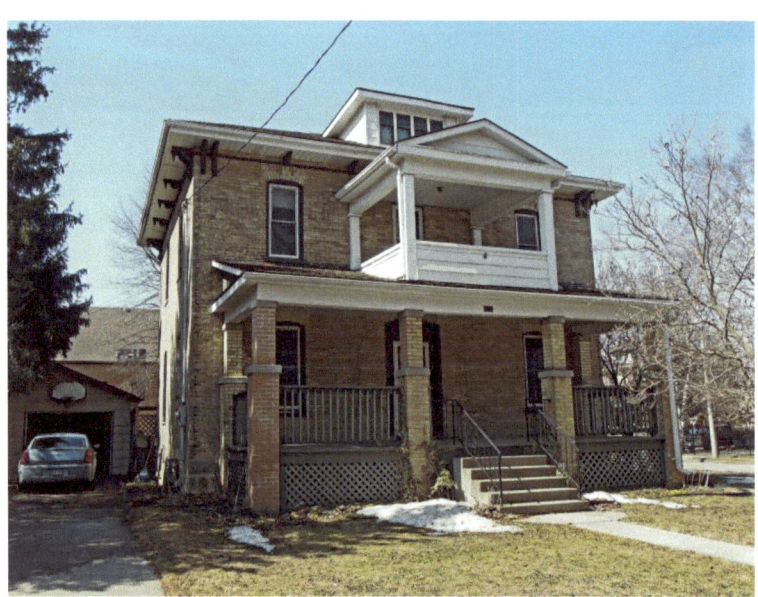

272 Peel Street – Italianate, dormer in attic, roofed-balcony
with pediment

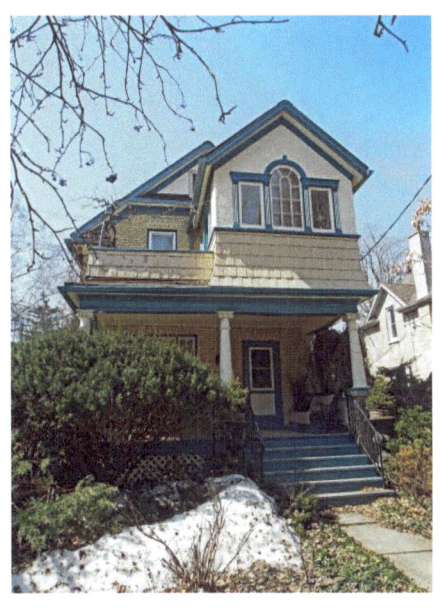

254 Peel Street – Edwardian, Palladian window

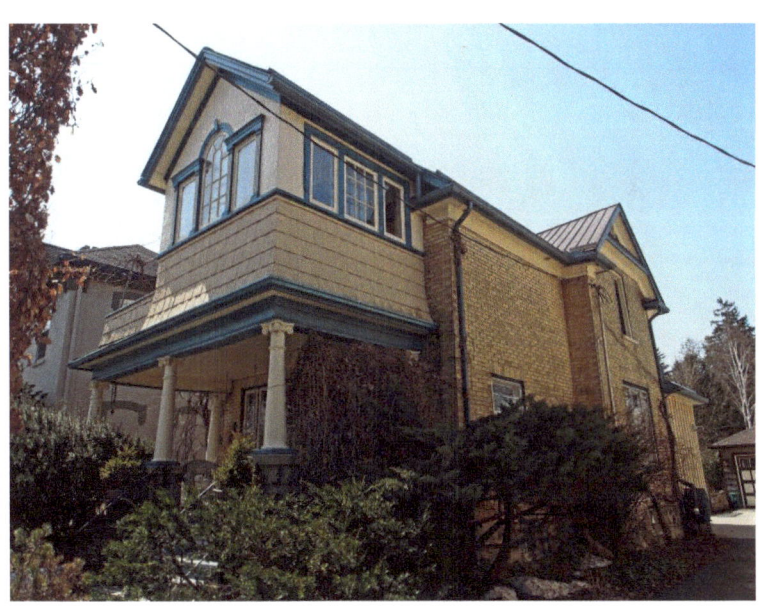

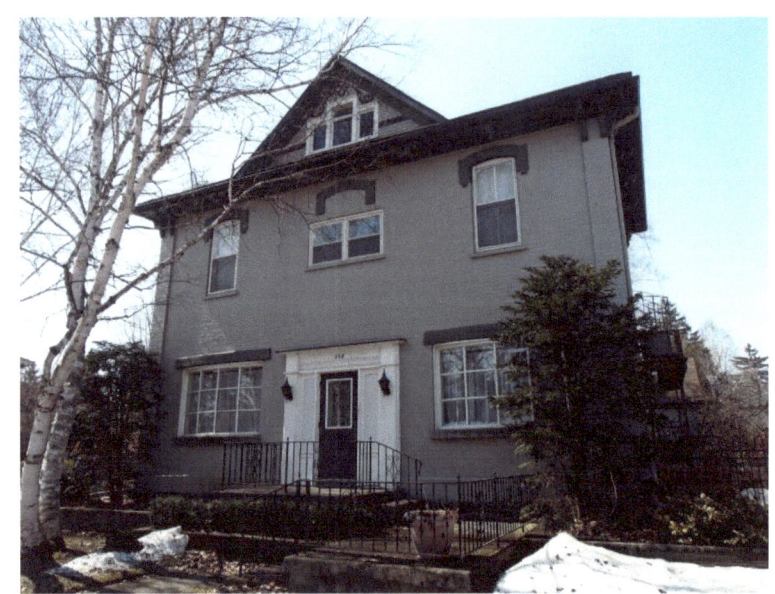

258 Peel Street – Italianate with gabled dormer on roof with Palladian window

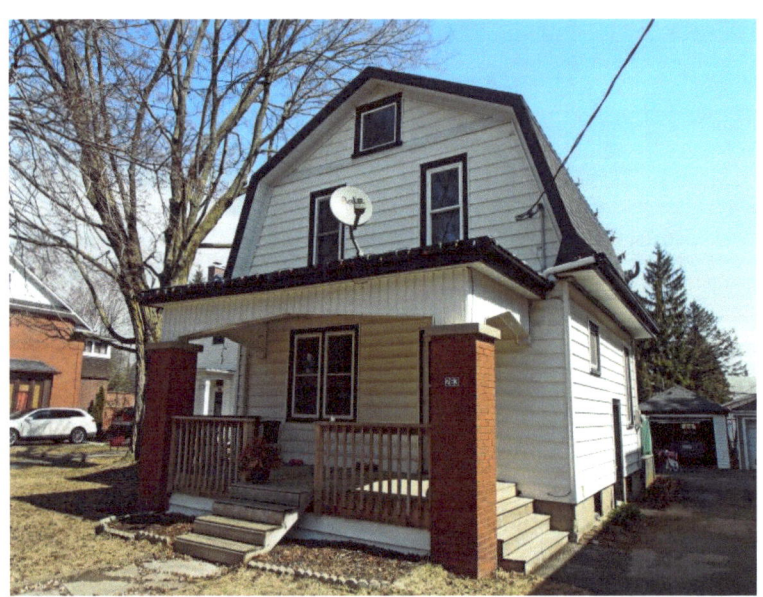

263 Peel Street

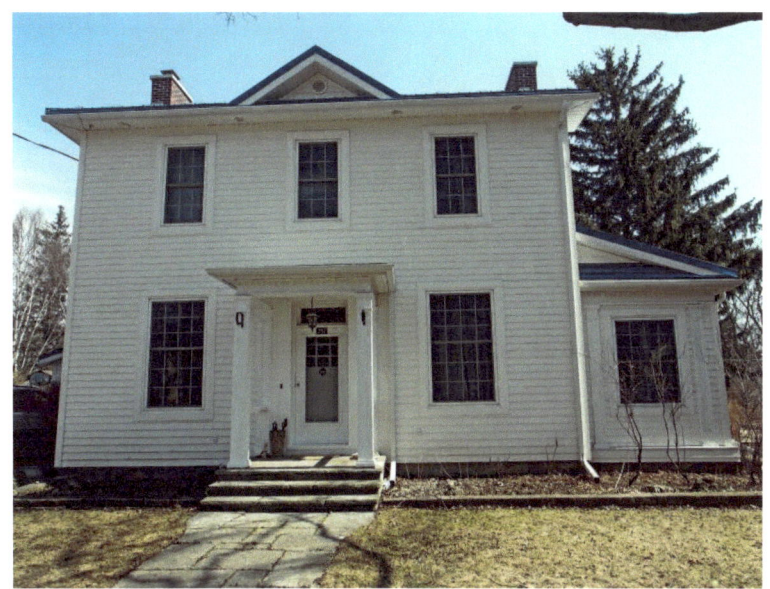

257 Peel Street - Georgian

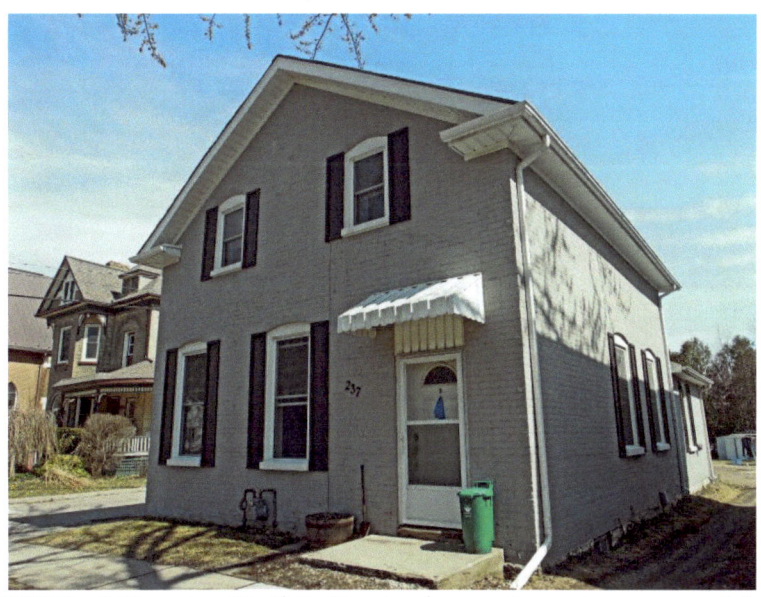

237 Peel Street – Gothic Revival, cornice return on gable

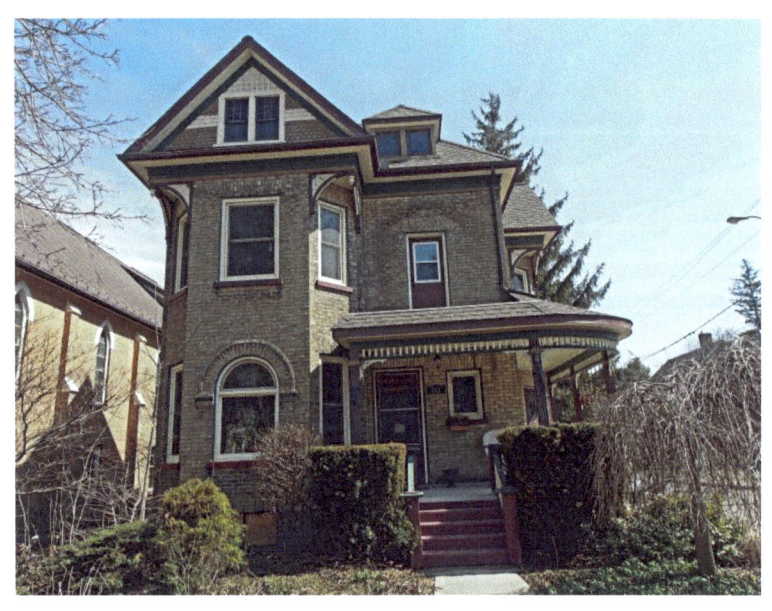

231 Peel Street – Queen Anne style

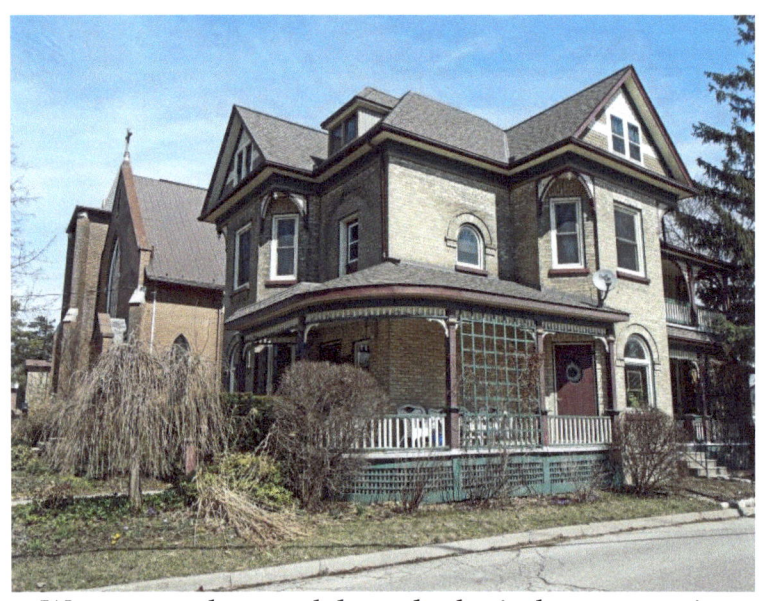

Wraparound verandah, arched window voussoirs

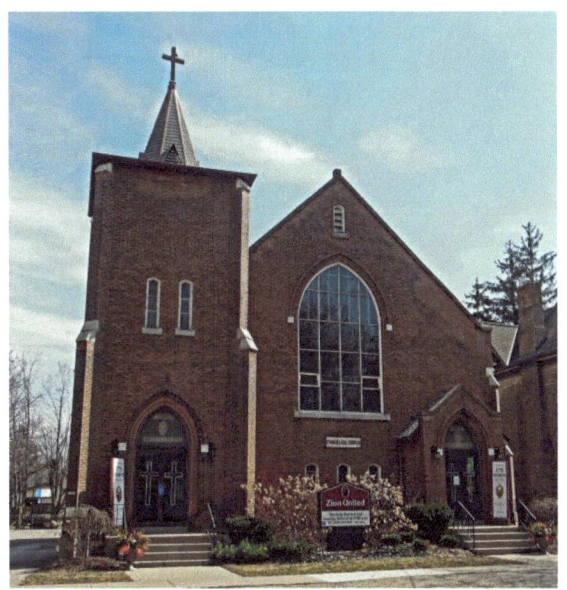

Zion United Church A.D. 1870

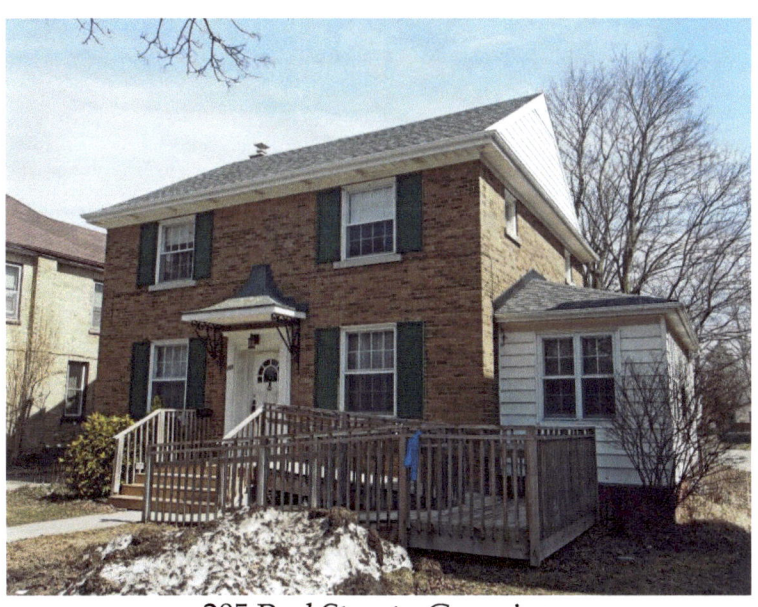

205 Peel Street - Georgian

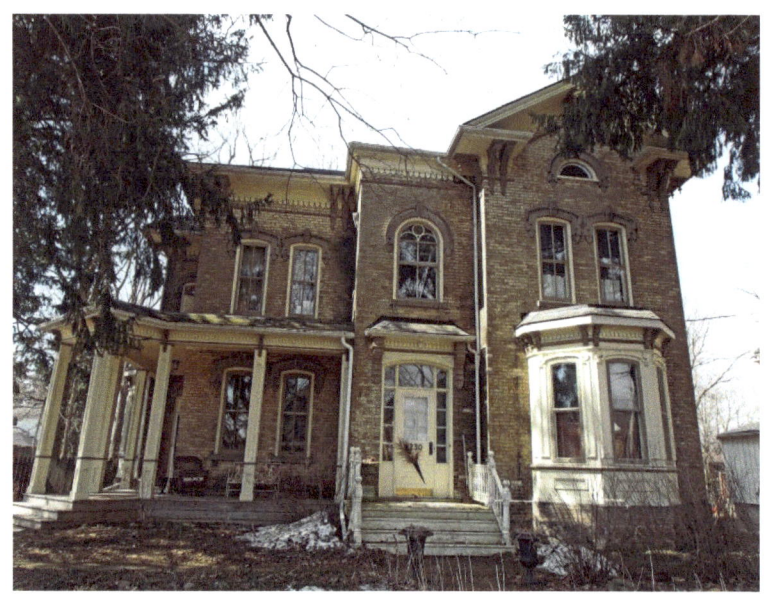

230 Peel Street – Italianate with two-storey frontispiece, and two-and-a-half storey with bay window on ground level, Paired cornice brackets, wraparound verandah

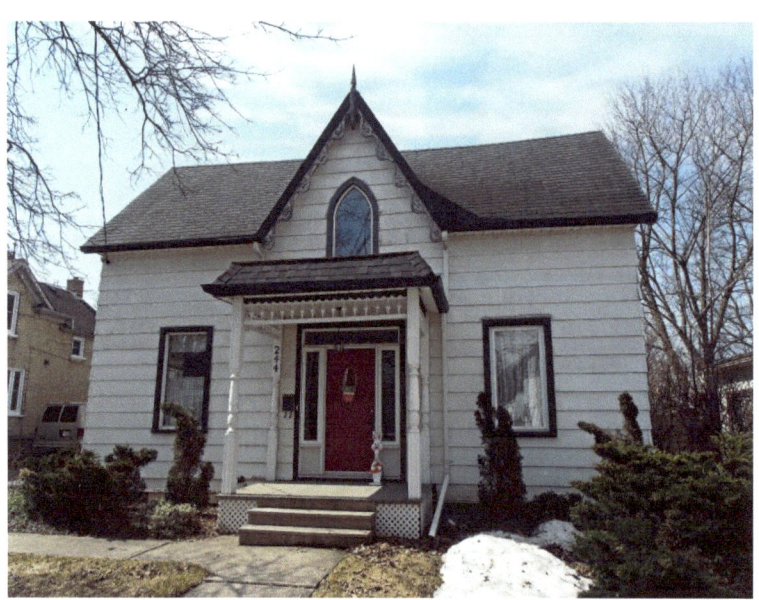

244 Peel Street – Gothic Revival Cottage

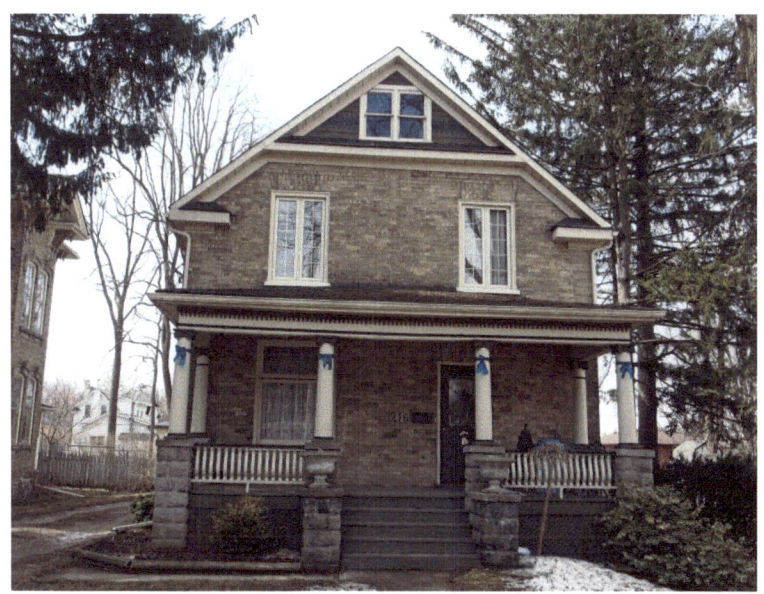

216 Peel Street – cornice return

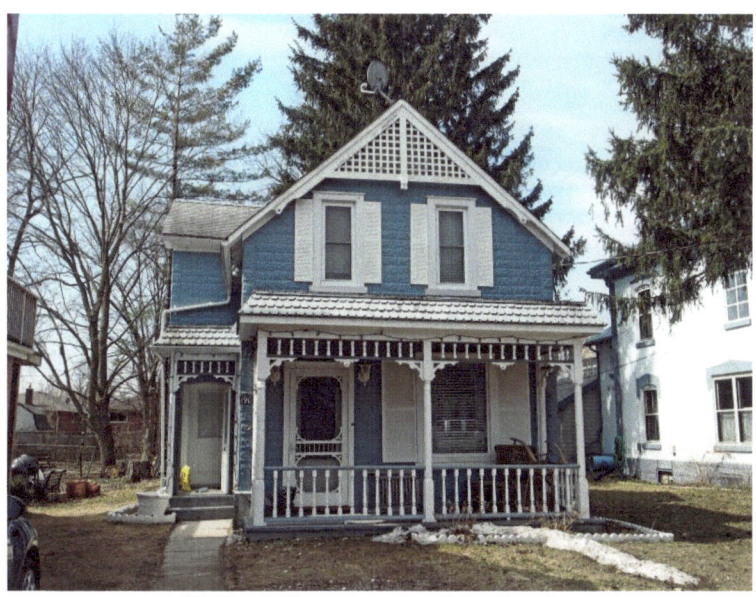

190 Peel Street – Gothic Revival

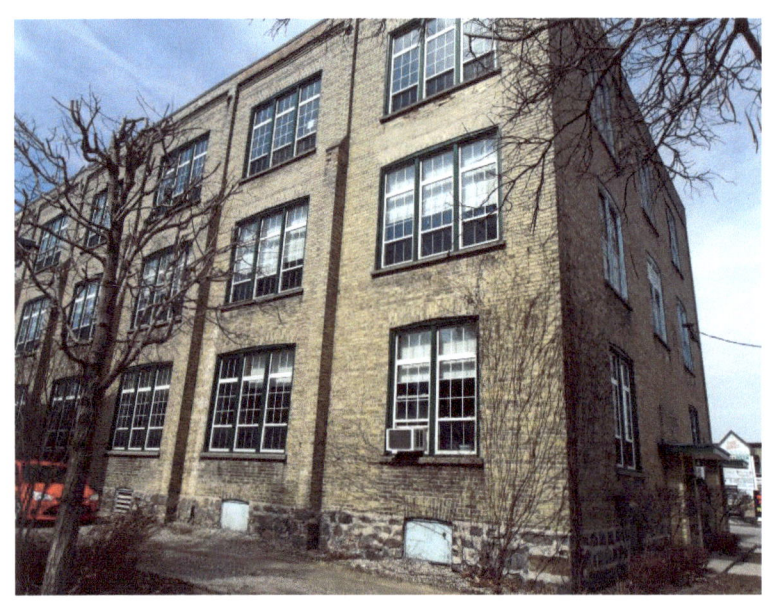

166 Peel Street – Hamburg Felt Boot Co. Limited

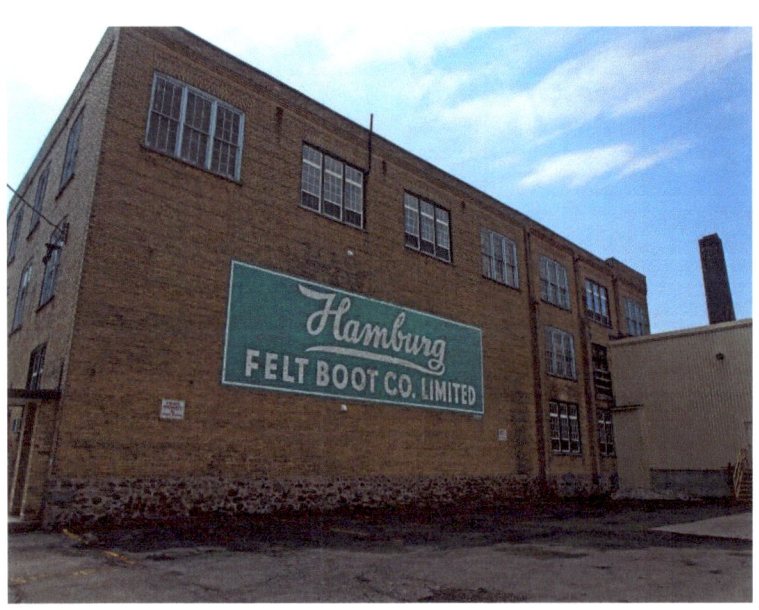

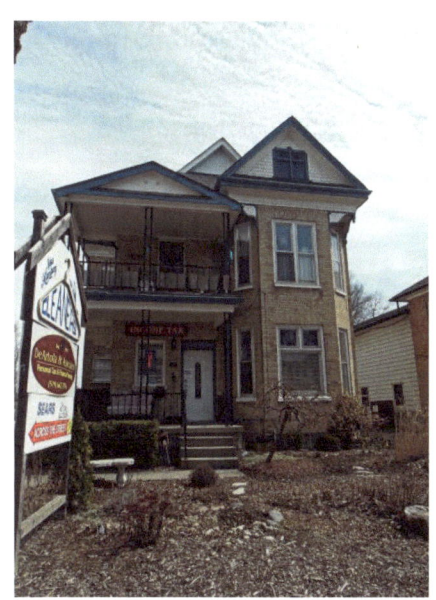

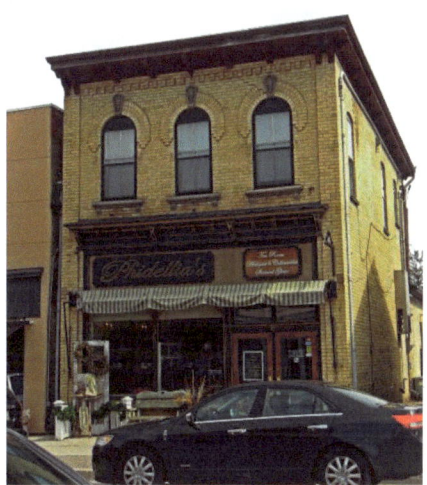

121 Peel Street - Italianate

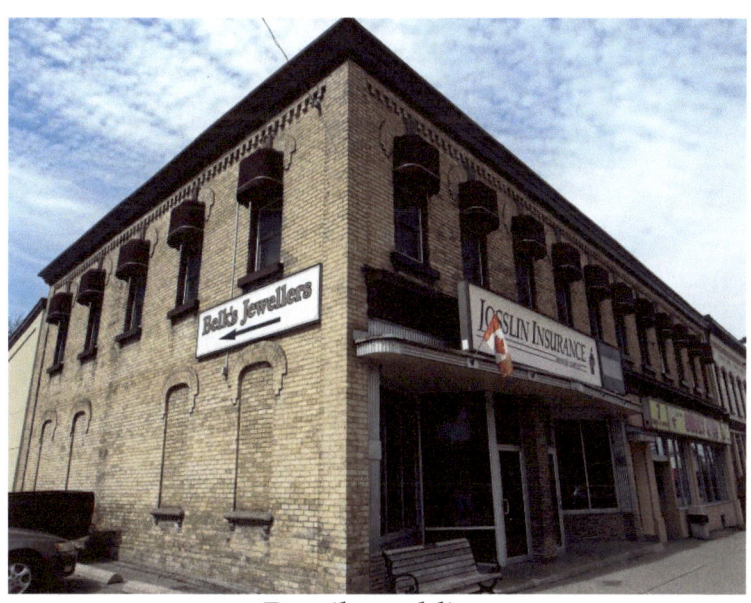

Dentil moulding

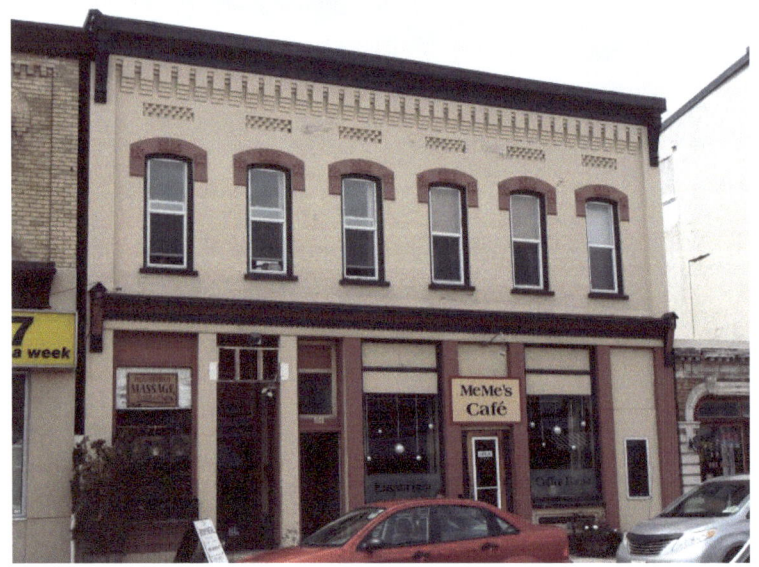

Dentil moulding

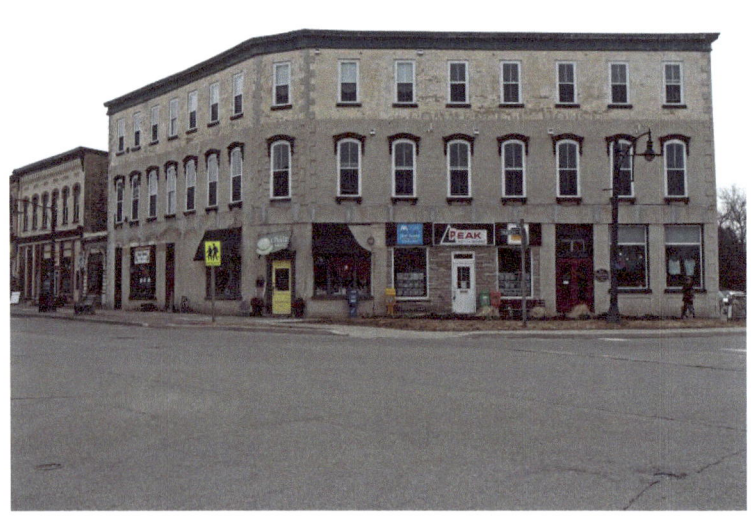

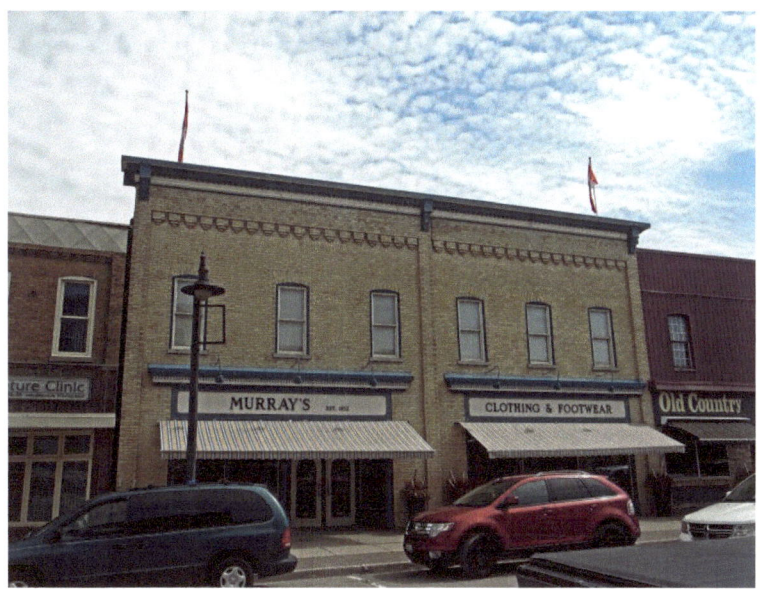

Dentil moulding, pilasters

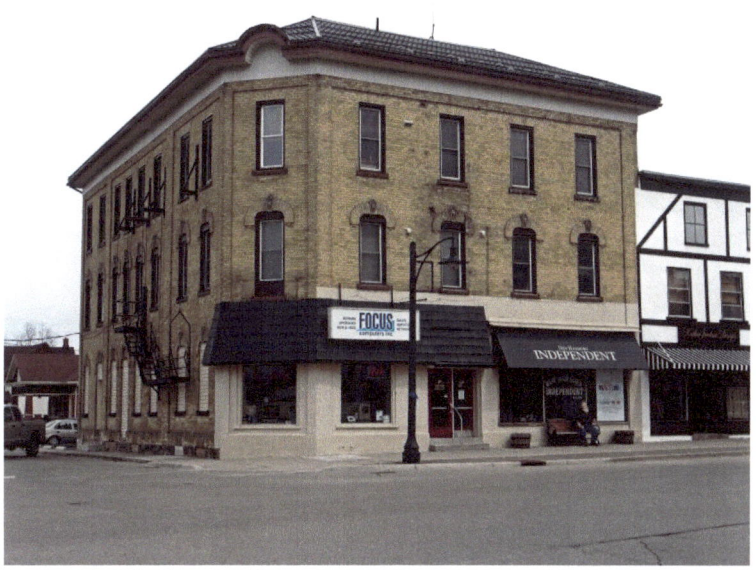

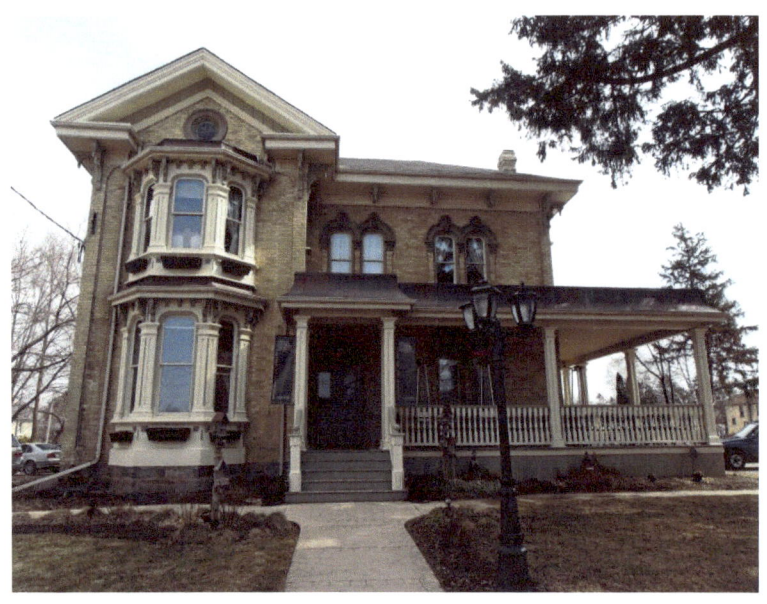

145 Peel Street – Italianate with two-and-a-half storey tower-like bay, wraparound verandah, decorative window voussoirs and keystones, single cornice brackets

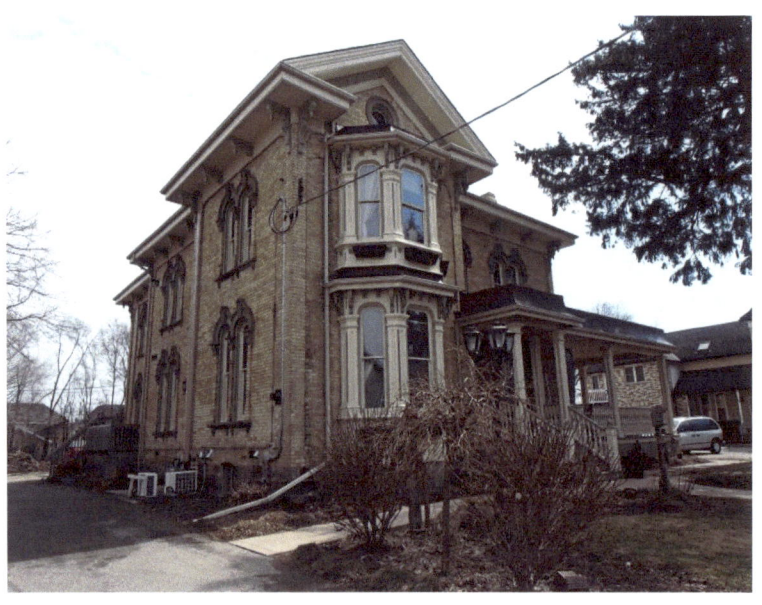

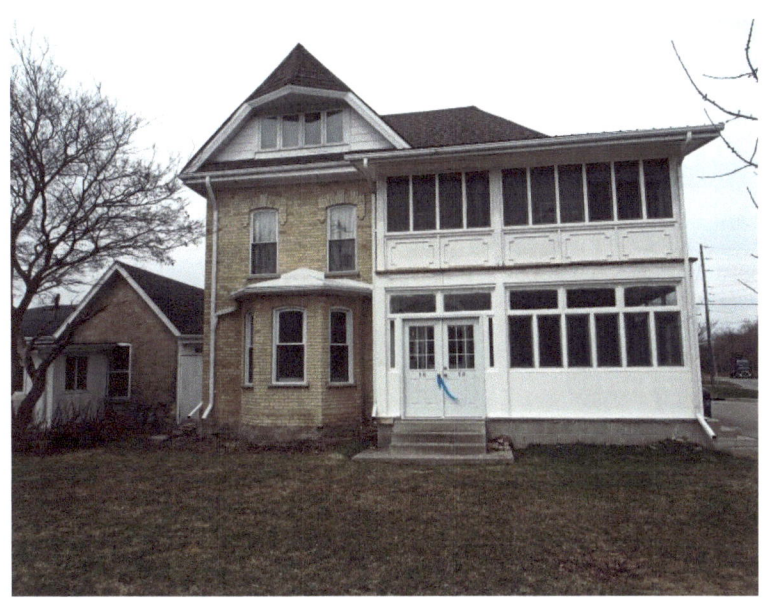

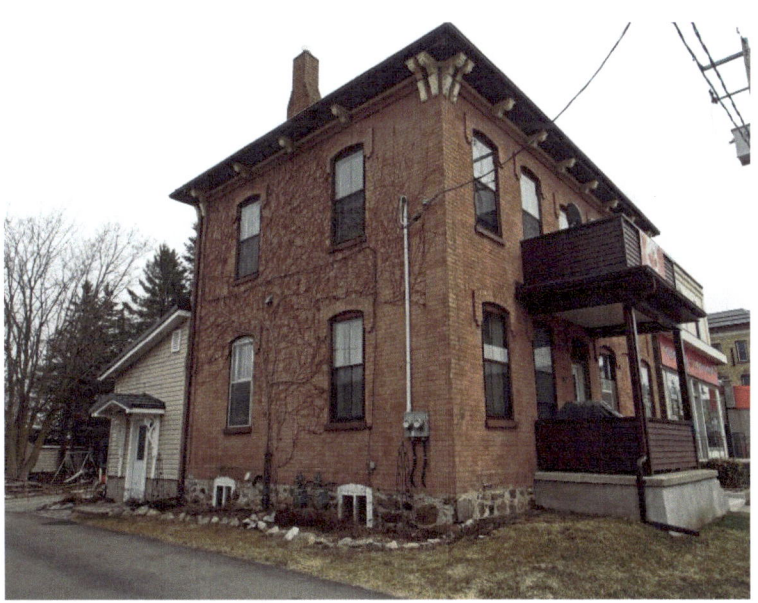

35 Peel Street – Italianate

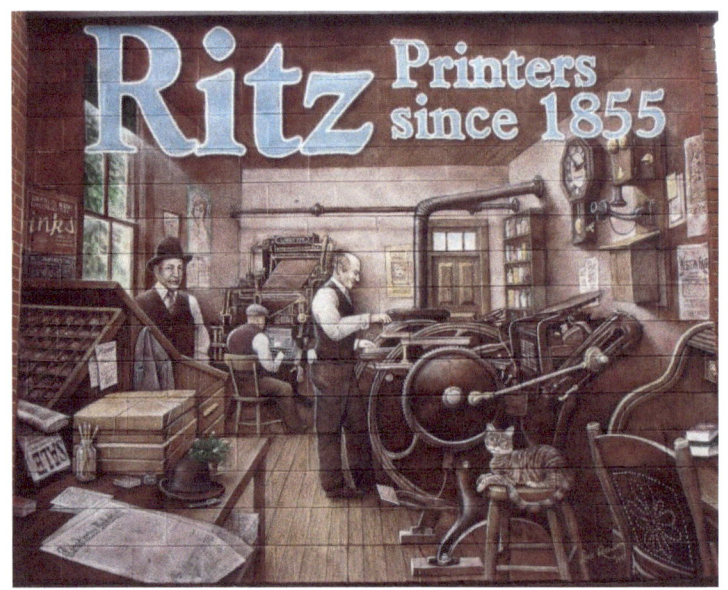
Print Shop Mural

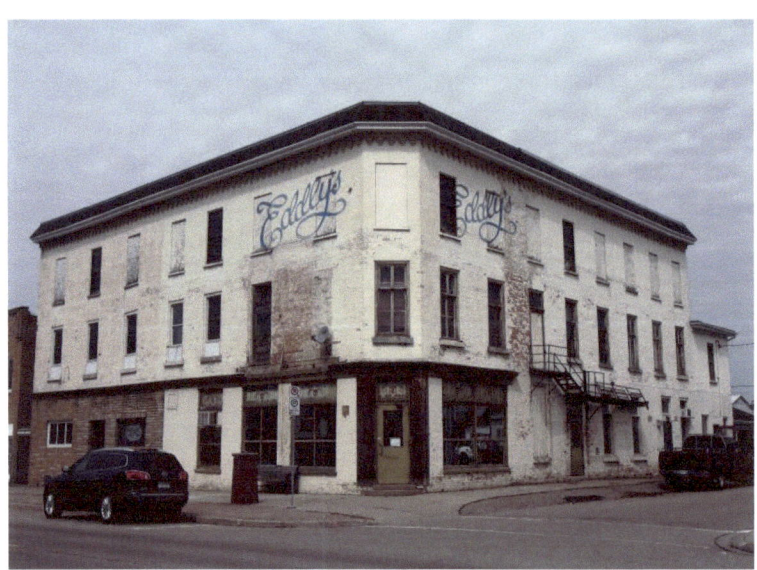
60 Huron Street – Imperial Hotel rebuilt in 1872 after a fire –
Italianate style - Eddly`s Restaurant and Bar

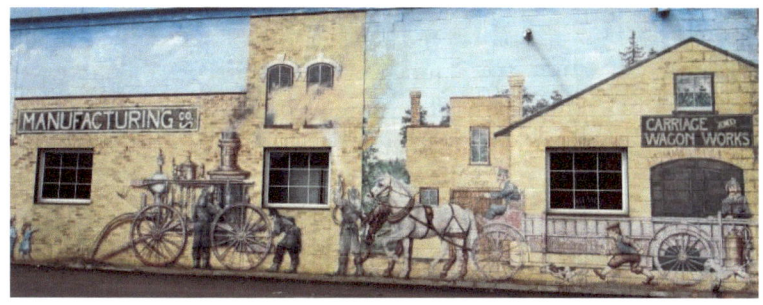

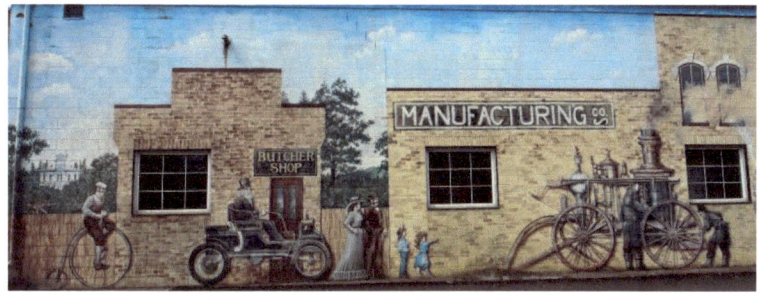

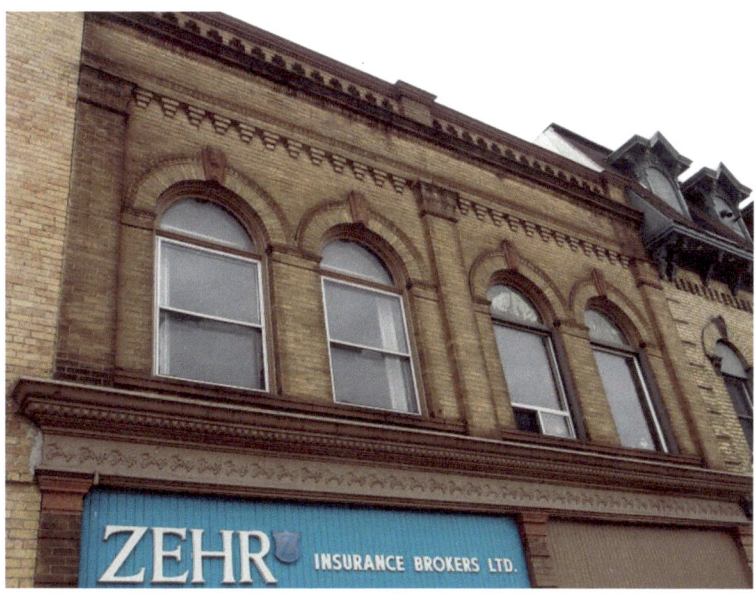

Dentil moulding, pilasters, arched window voussoirs with keystones

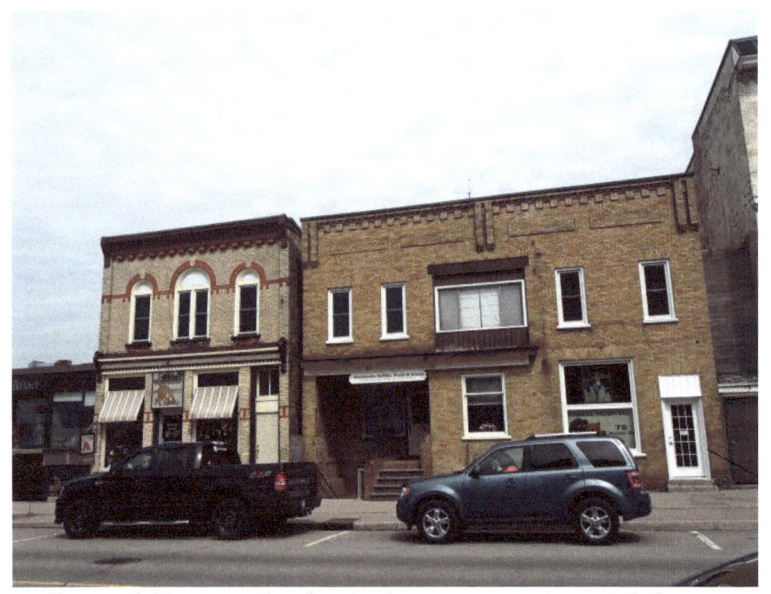

Dentil moulding, arched window voussoirs with keystones

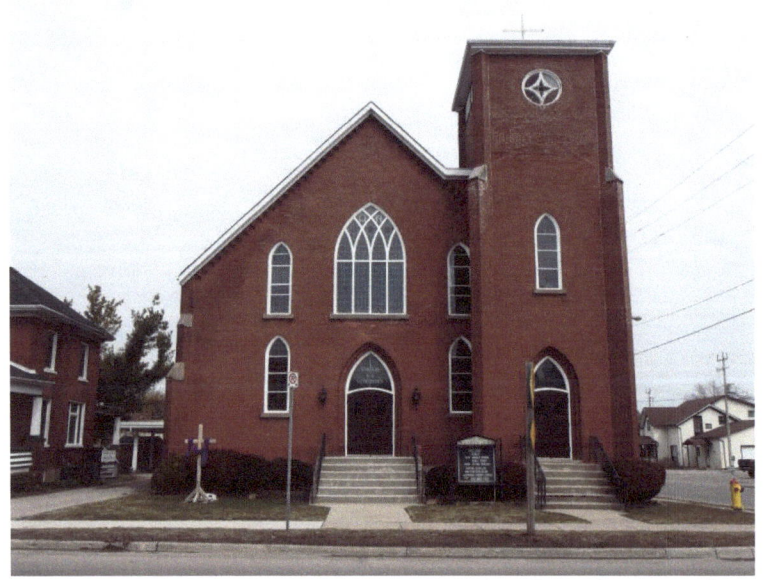

144 Huron Street - St. Peter`s Evangelical Lutheran Church
c. 1910 – Gothic Revival style

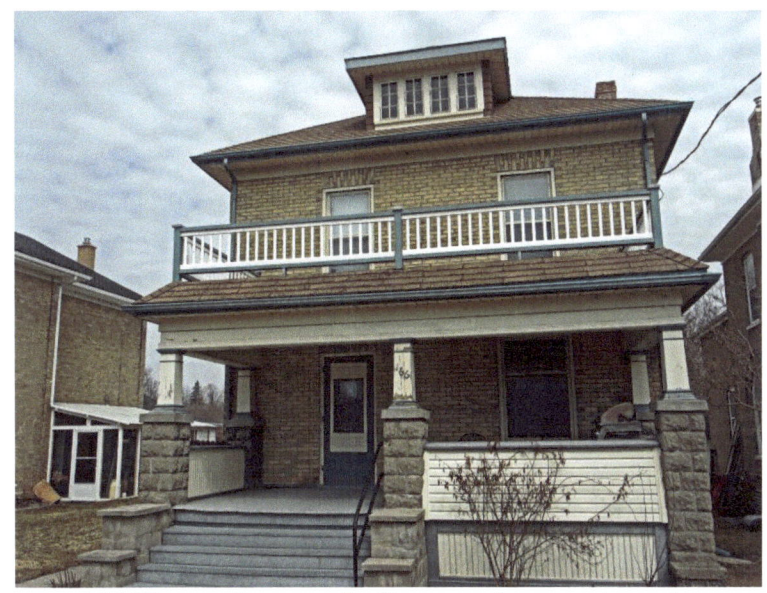

166 Huron Street – Italianate, dormer in attic,
Second floor wraparound balcony/verandah

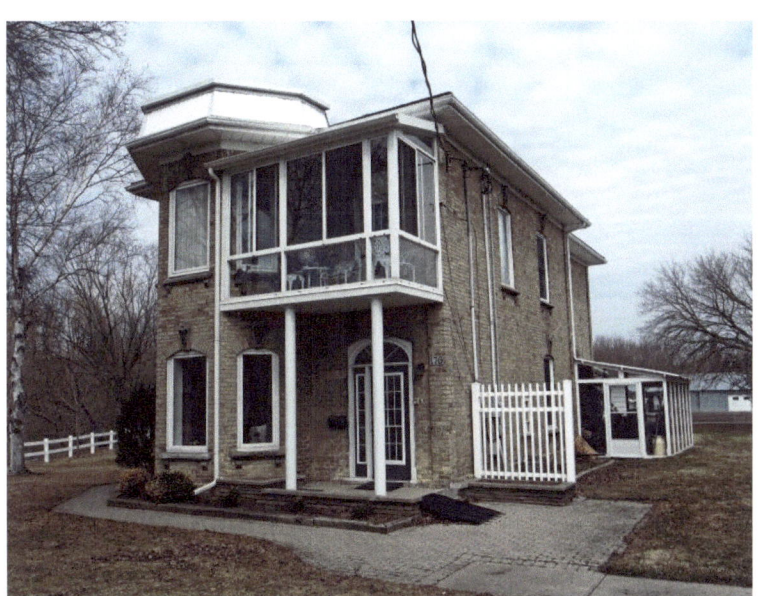

176 Huron Street - Italianate

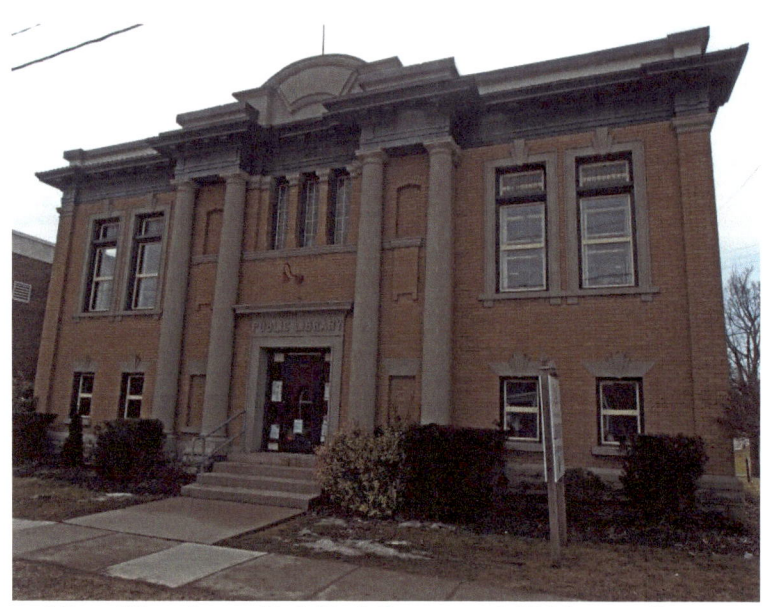

New Hamburg Public Library – 145 Huron Street
Beaux Arts/Classical Revival style

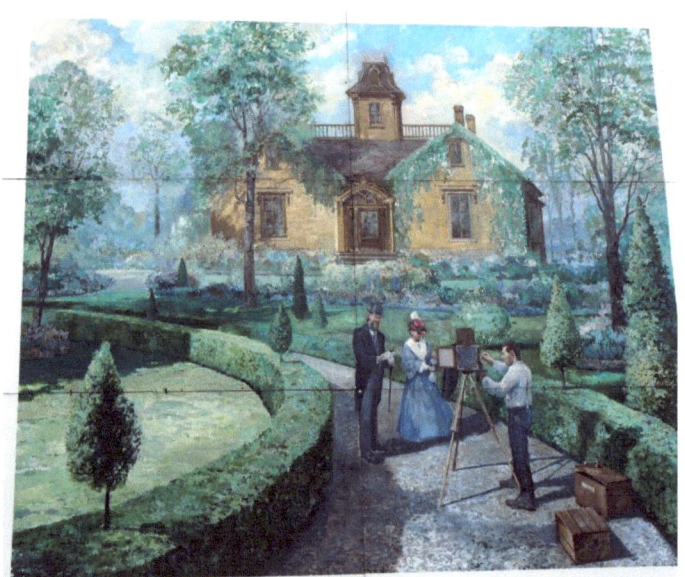

Mural

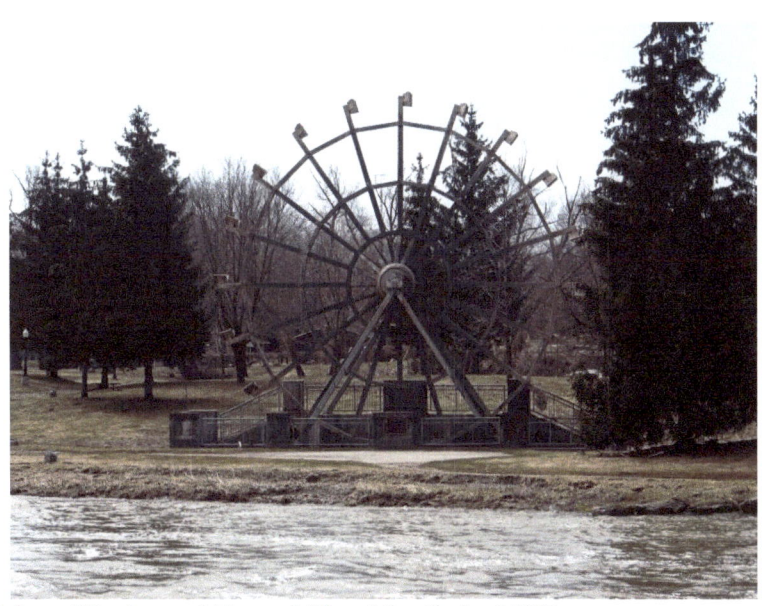

65 foot Heritage Water Wheel built in 1990 to commemorate
the early water-powered industries located along
the Nith River

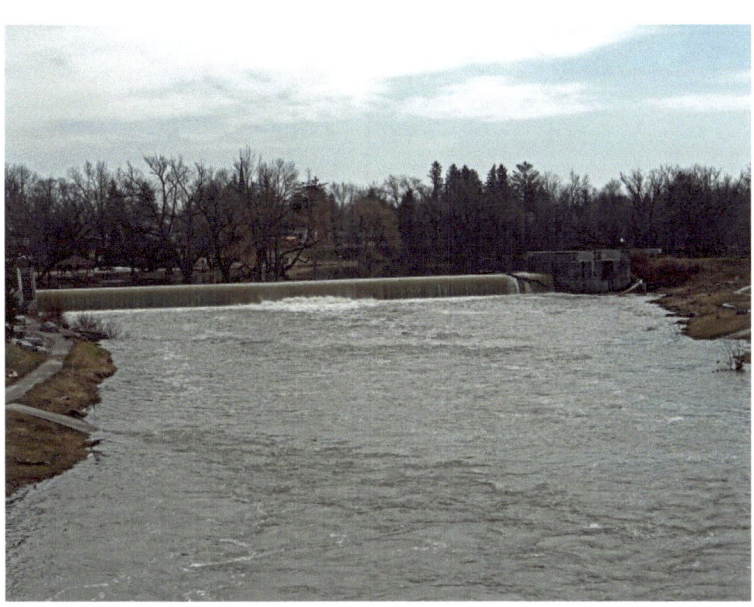

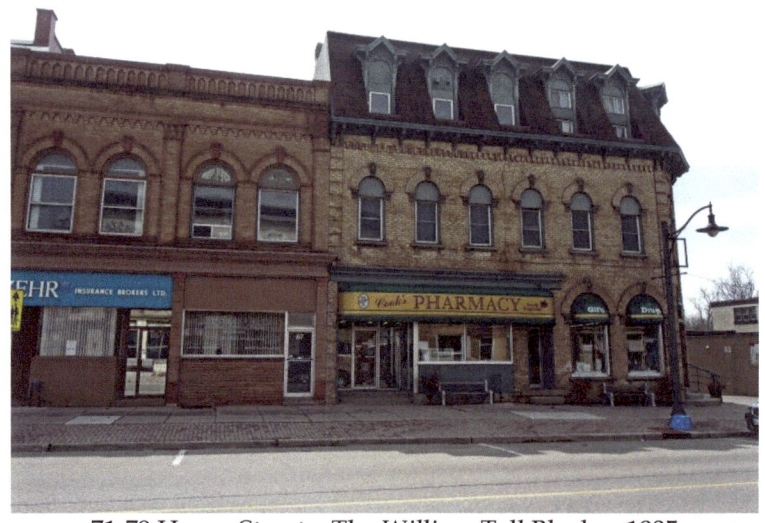

71-79 Huron Street – The William Tell Block c. 1885
– Second Empire architecture with
"grape motif" keystone over the windows

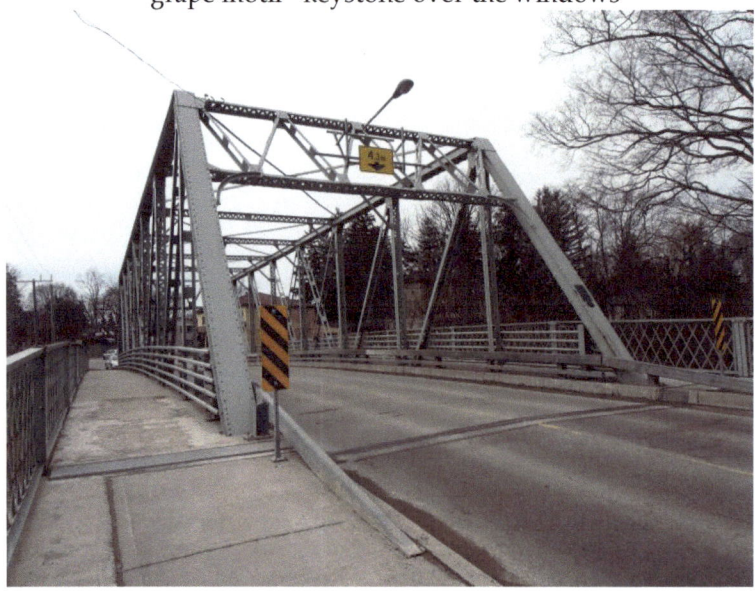

Hartman Bridge is a steel Pratt truss bridge built during the Great Depression by the Hamilton Bridge Company. The first wooden bridge was built here about 1845. It was named after the Hartman family who owned and donated the land on one side of the river.

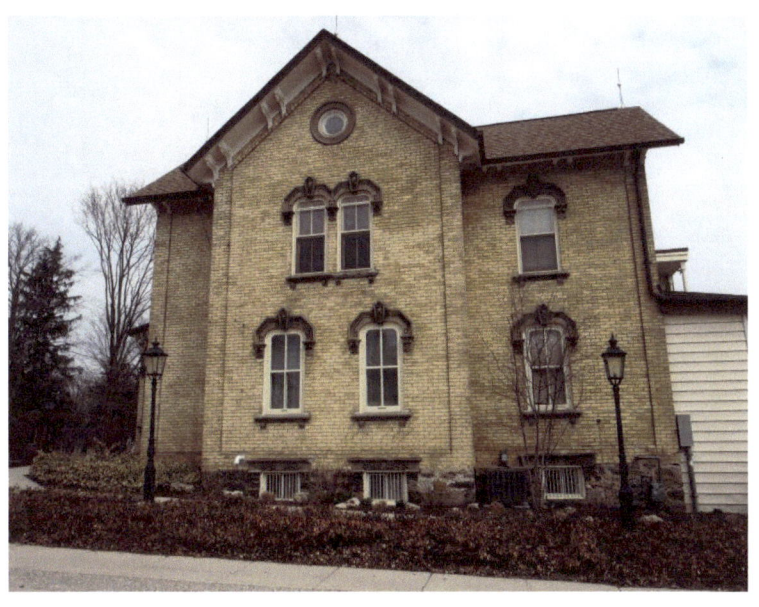

291 Huron Street – Mark Jutzi Funeral Home

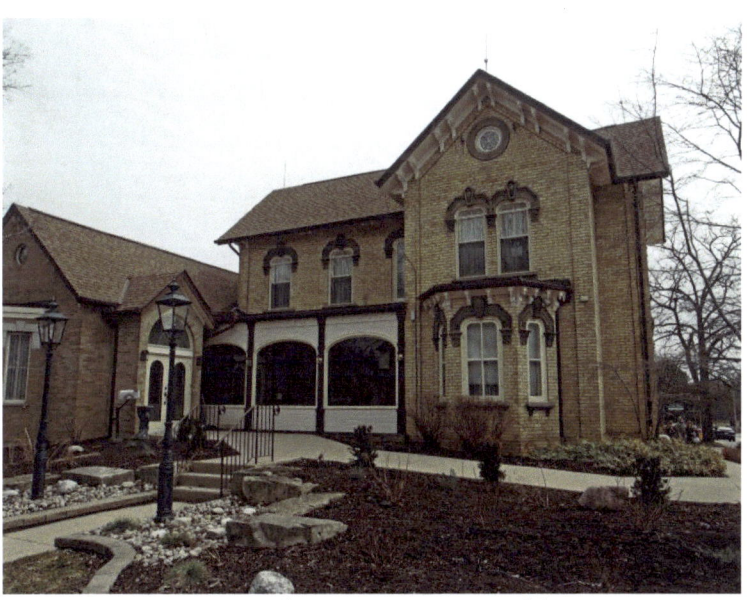

Decorative window voussoirs and keystones

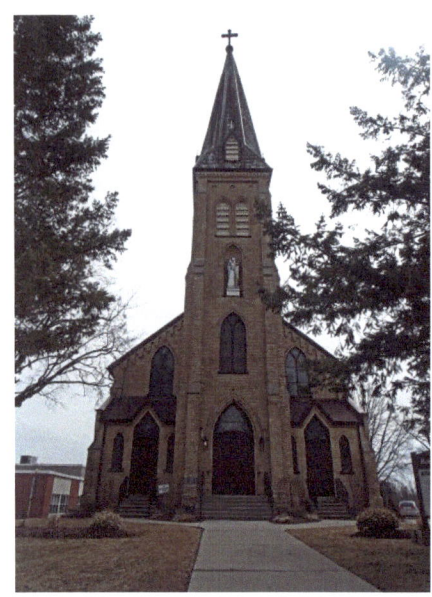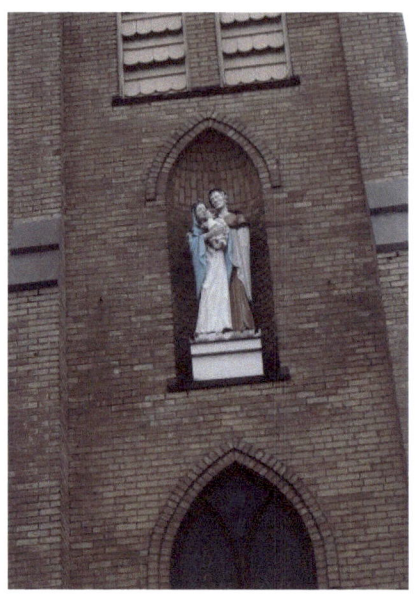

Holy Family Roman Catholic Church

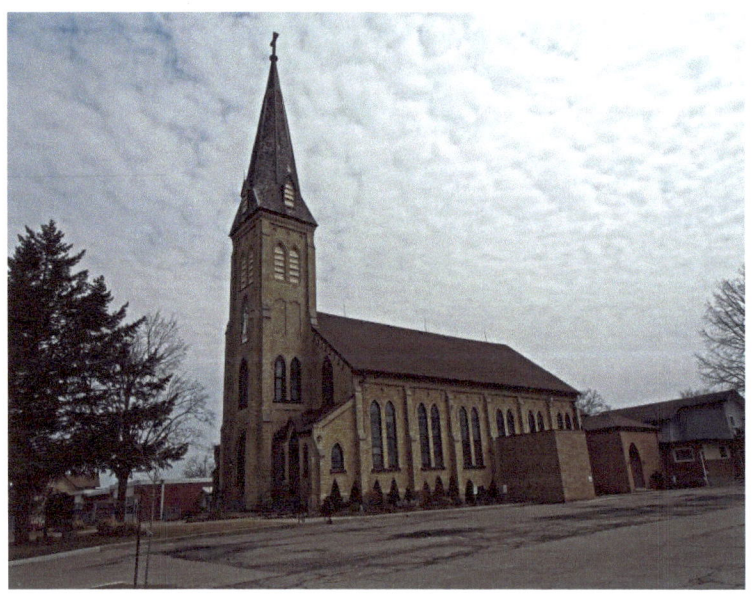

Lancet windows

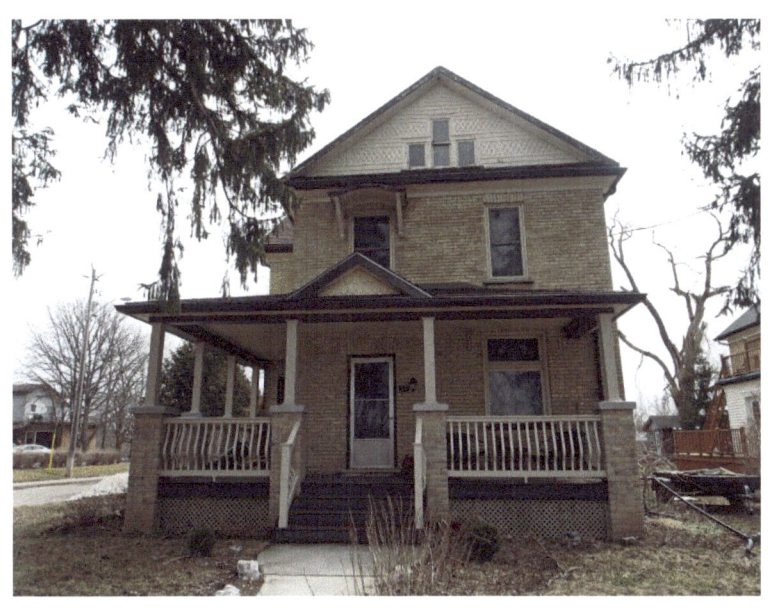

347 Huron Street – Edwardian, Palladian window, pediment above doorway

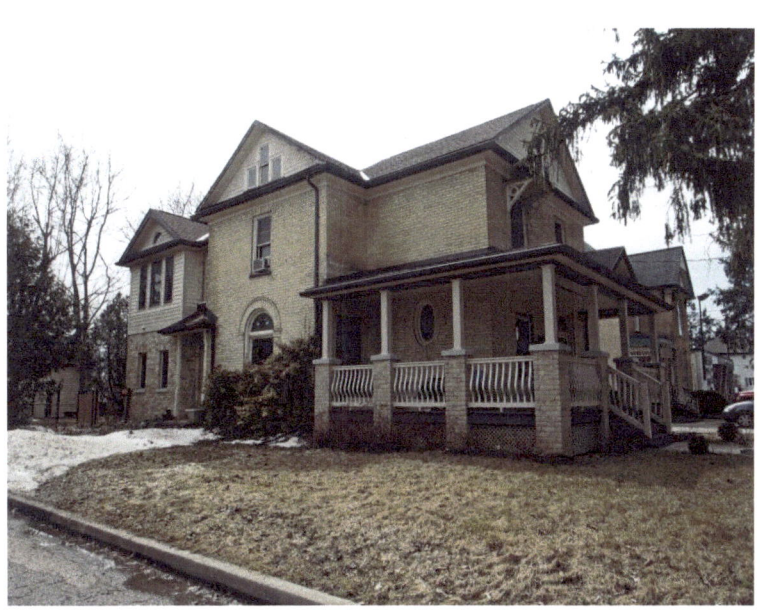

Romanesque style arched window voussoirs

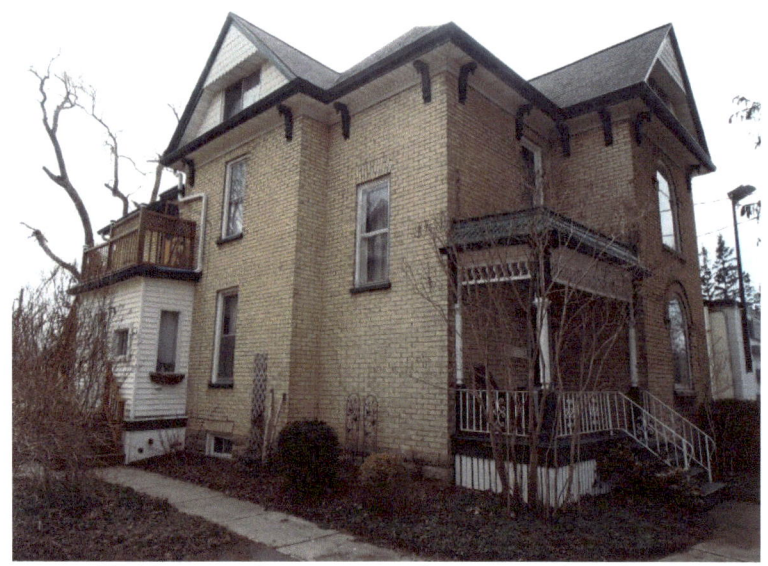

551 Huron Street – single cornice brackets

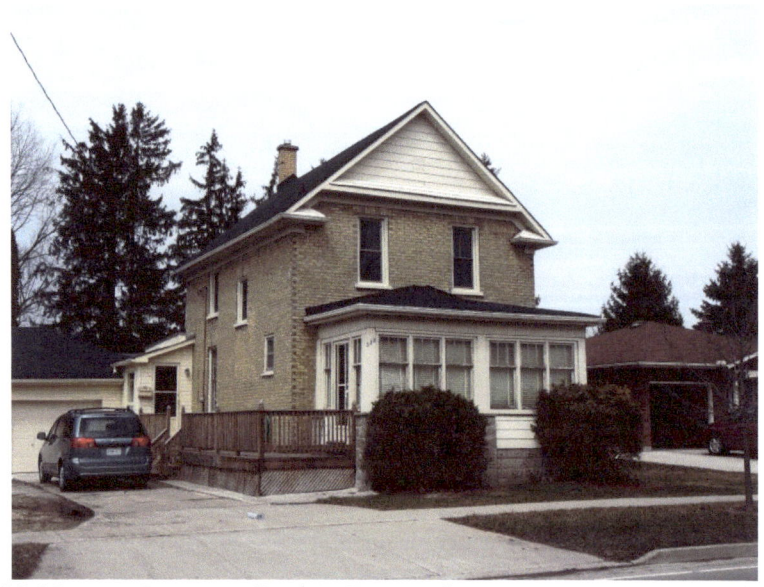

328 Huron Street – Gothic Revival, cornice return on gable

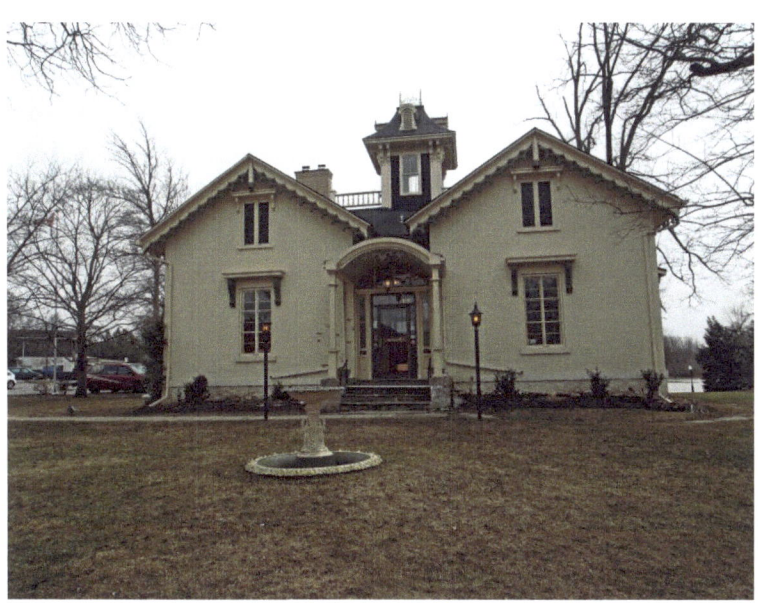

17 Huron Street – The William Scott House – Gothic style with Italianate features was built about 1846. Belvedere on roof, Vergeboard trim on gables with finials
Now The Waterlot Restaurant

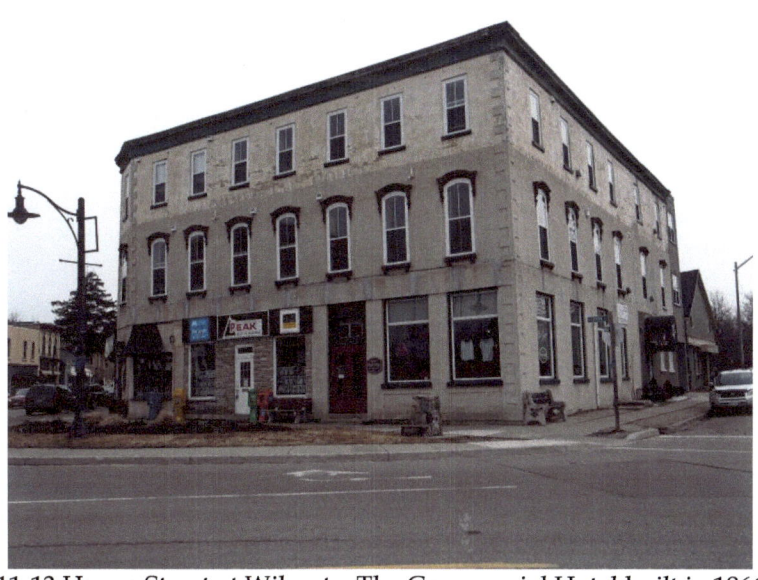

11-13 Huron Street at Wilmot – The Commercial Hotel built in 1866 – Italianate, corner quoins

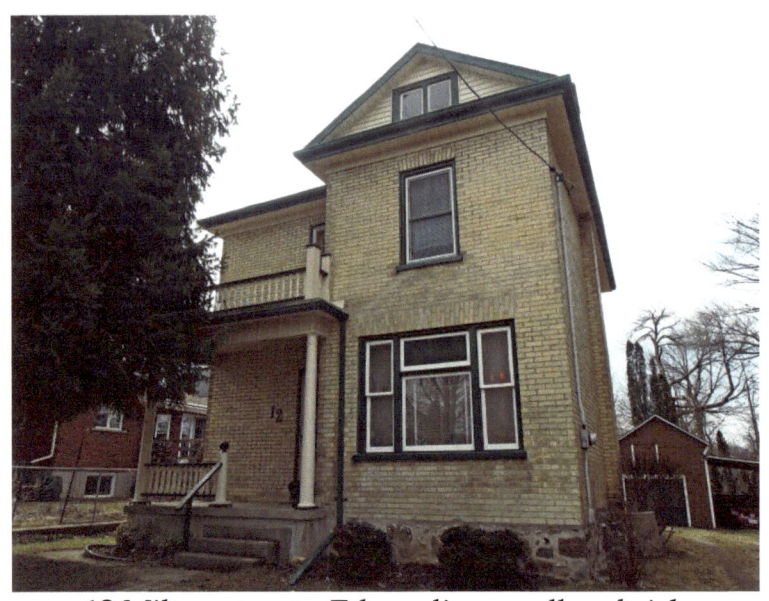

12 Milton street – Edwardian – yellow brick

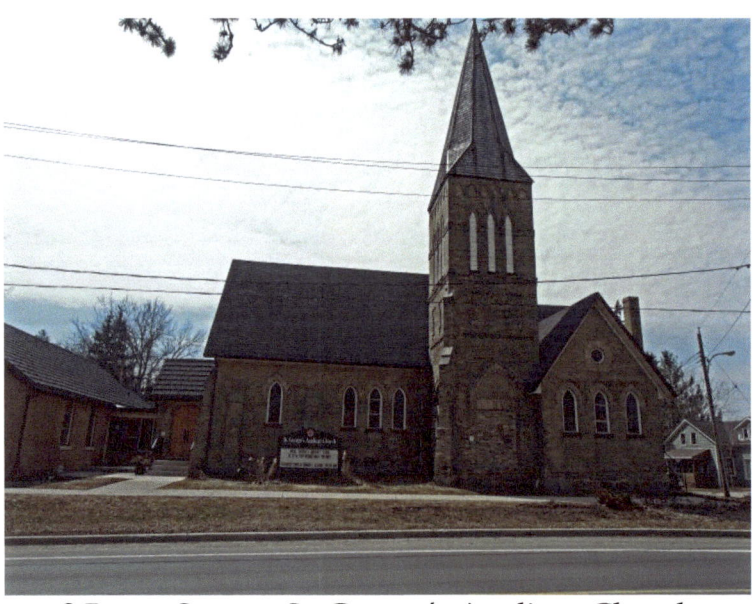

3 Byron Street – St. George's Anglican Church

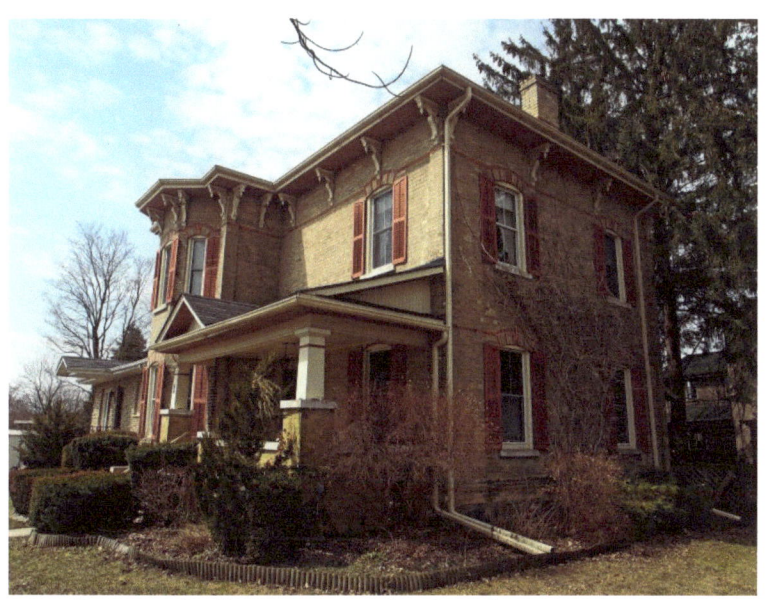

2 Byron Street – Italianate, cornice brackets, two-storey tower-like bay, dichromatic brickwork

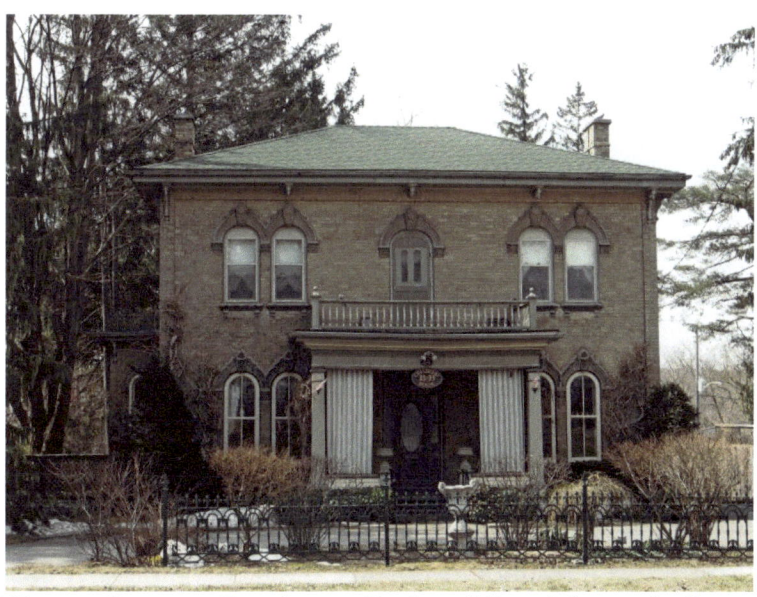

54 Byron Street – Cranberry Bed and Breakfast - Italianate, hip roof, decorative window voussoirs and keystones

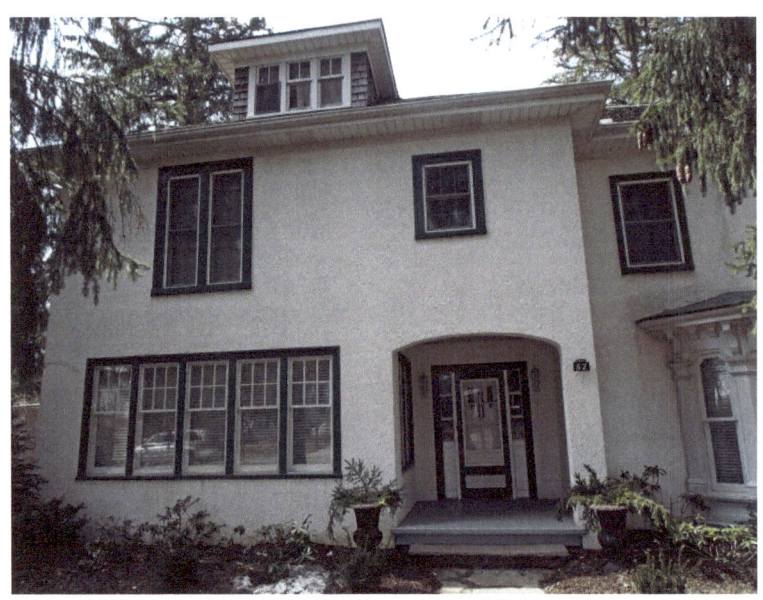

62 Byron Street – Italianate with roof dormer

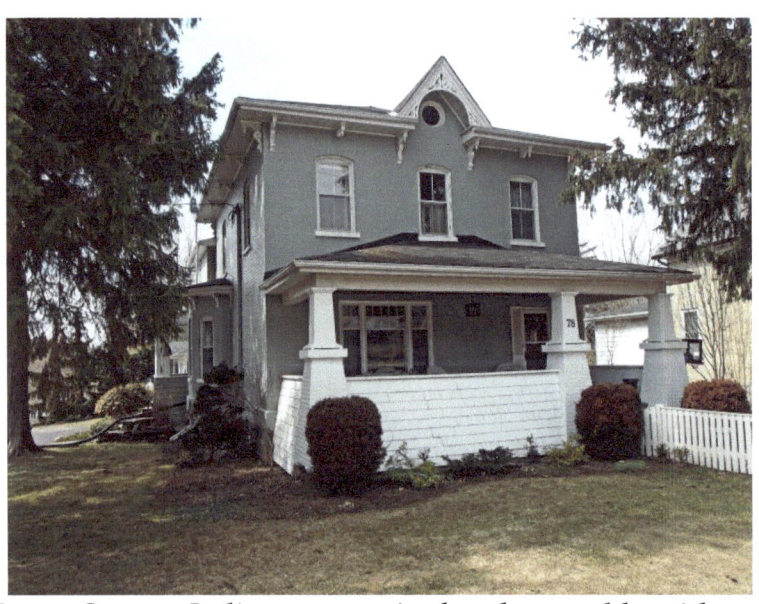

78 Byron Street – Italianate, cornice brackets, gable with round window, Vergeboard trim

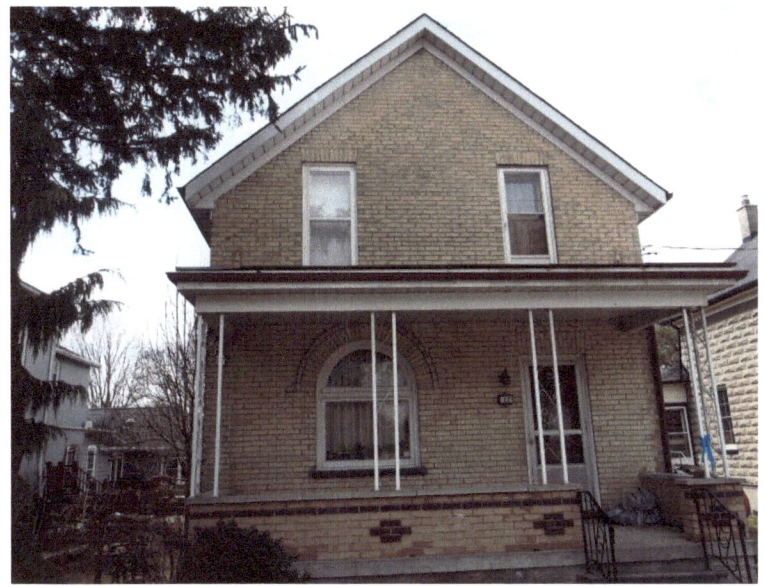

82 Byron Street – Gothic with Romanesque style window arch

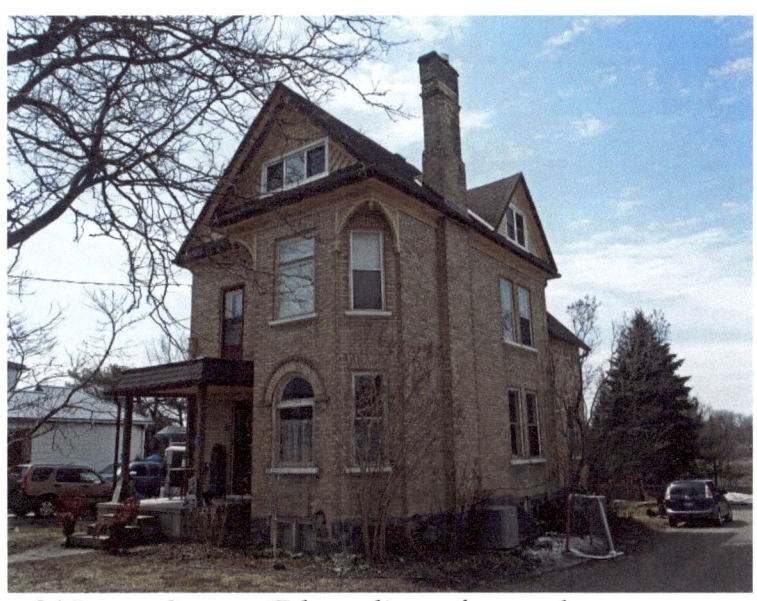

96 Byron Street – Edwardian – fretwork on corners

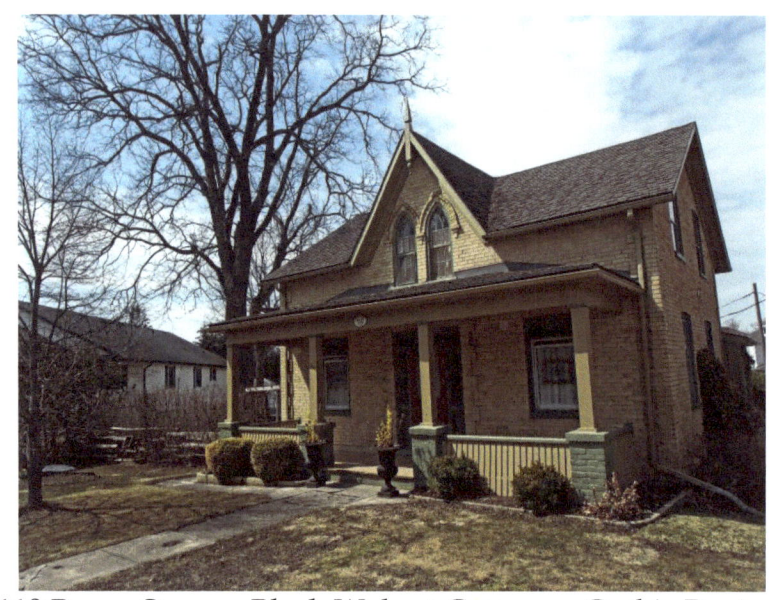

110 Byron Street – Black Walnut Cottage – Gothic Revival
– twin lancet windows in gable with finial

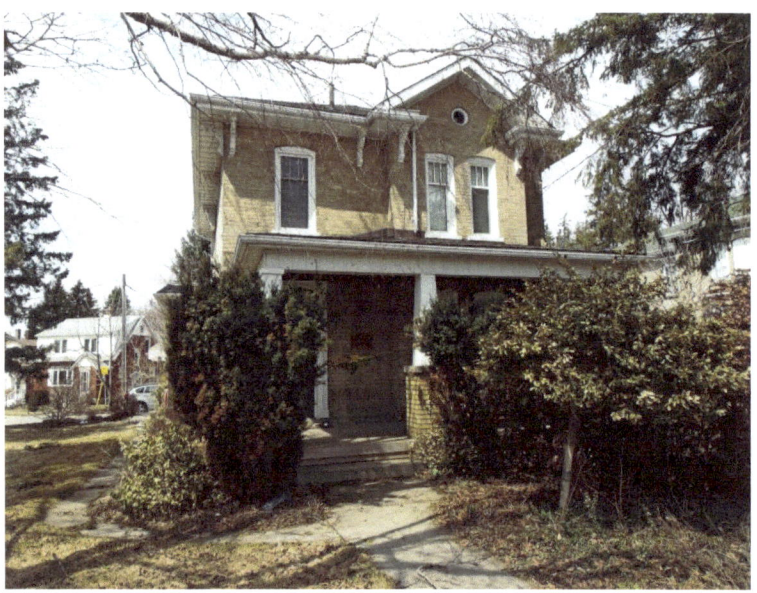

120 Byron Street – Italianate with two-and-a-half storey
frontispiece with cornice return on gable, cornice brackets

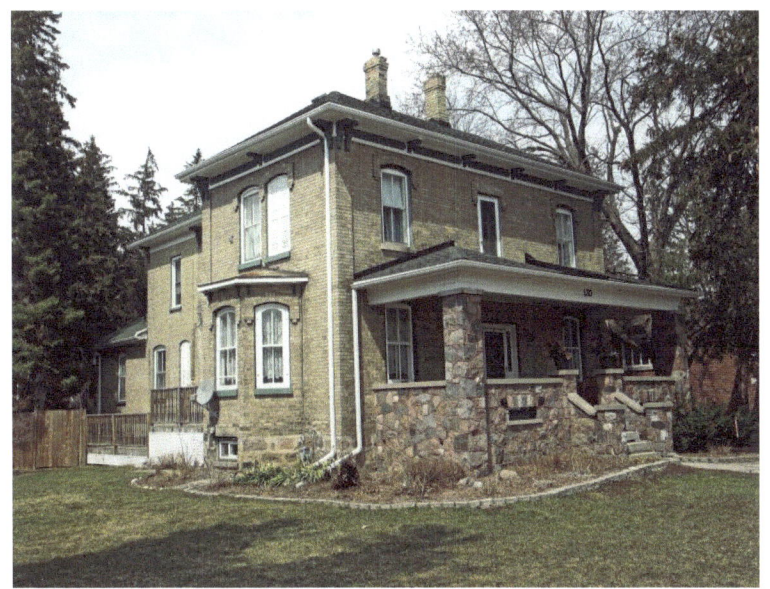

130 Byron Street - Italianate

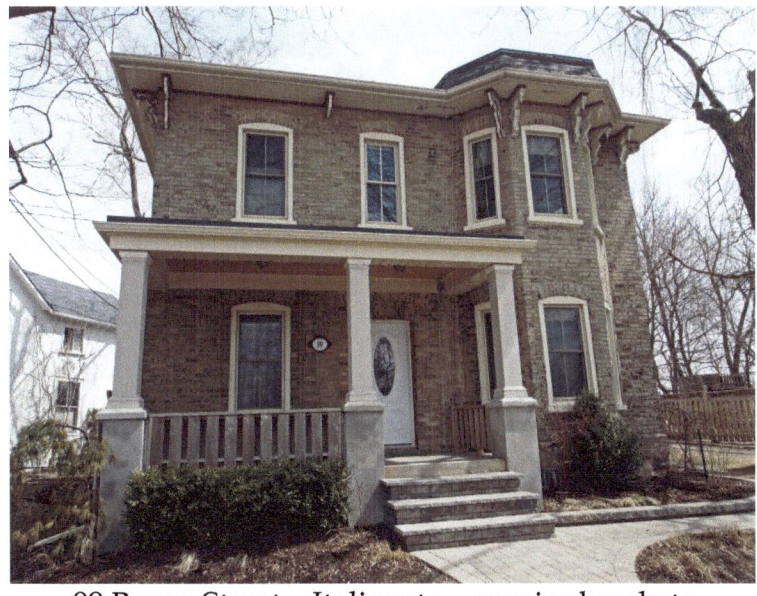

99 Byron Street – Italianate – cornice brackets

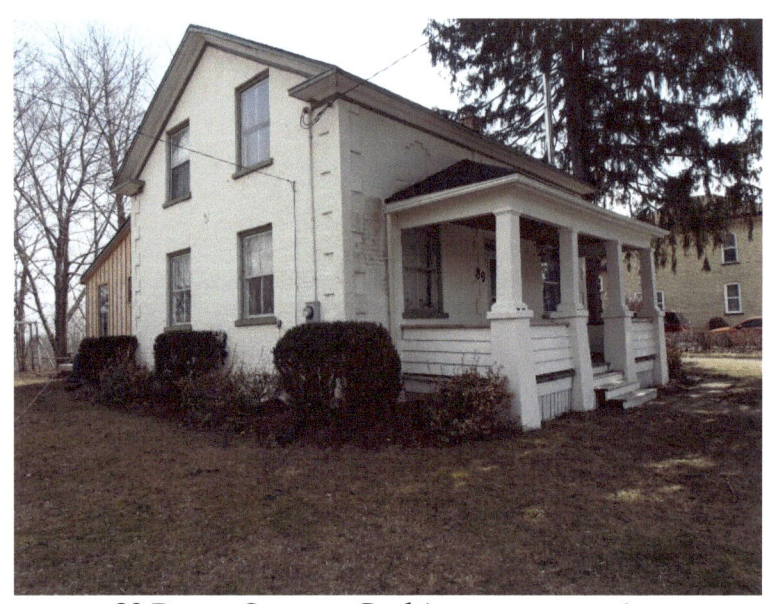

89 Byron Street – Gothic - corner quoins

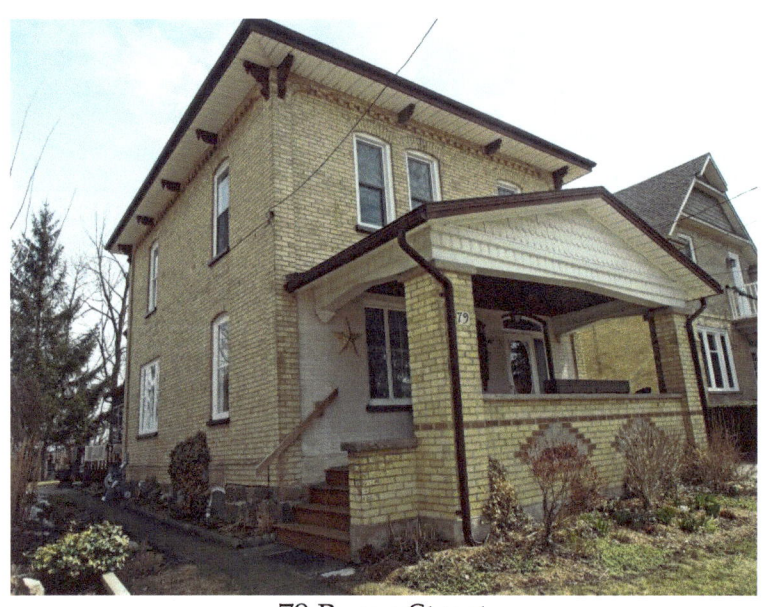

79 Byron Street

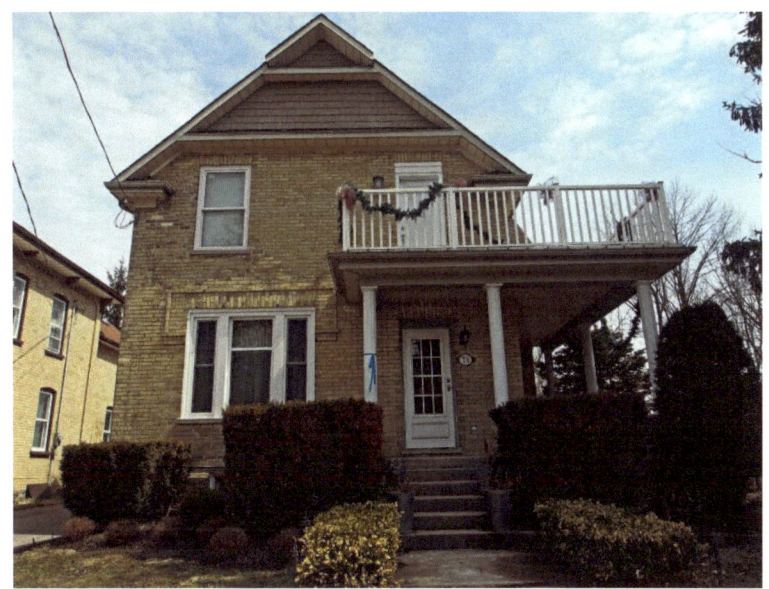

75 Byron Street – Gothic – yellow brick

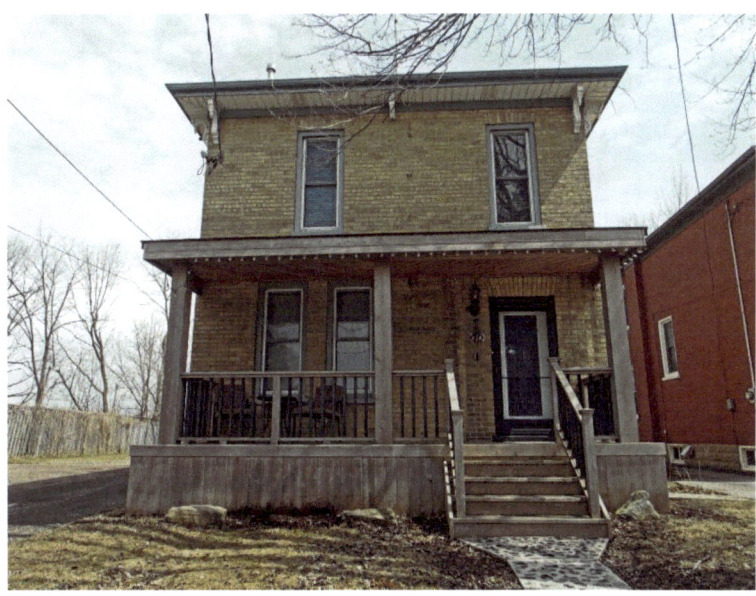

65 Byron Street – Italianate – cornice brackets, yellow brick

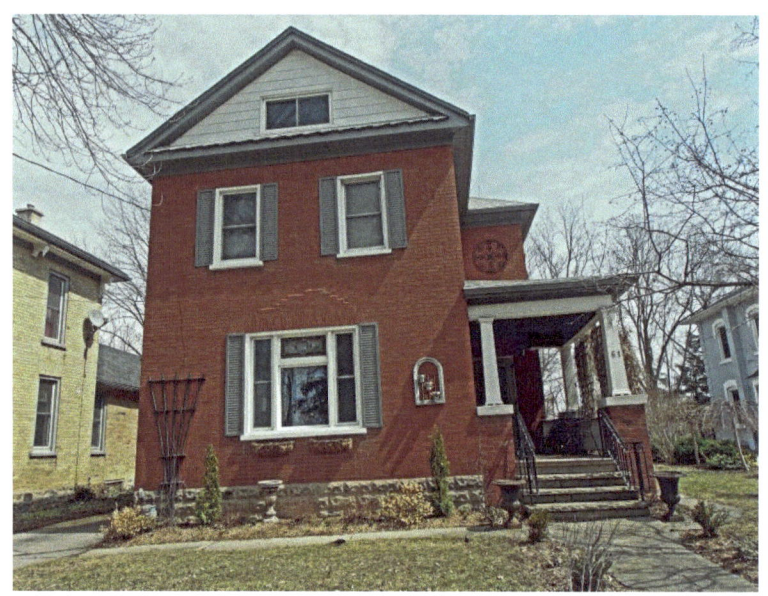

61 Byron Street - Edwardian

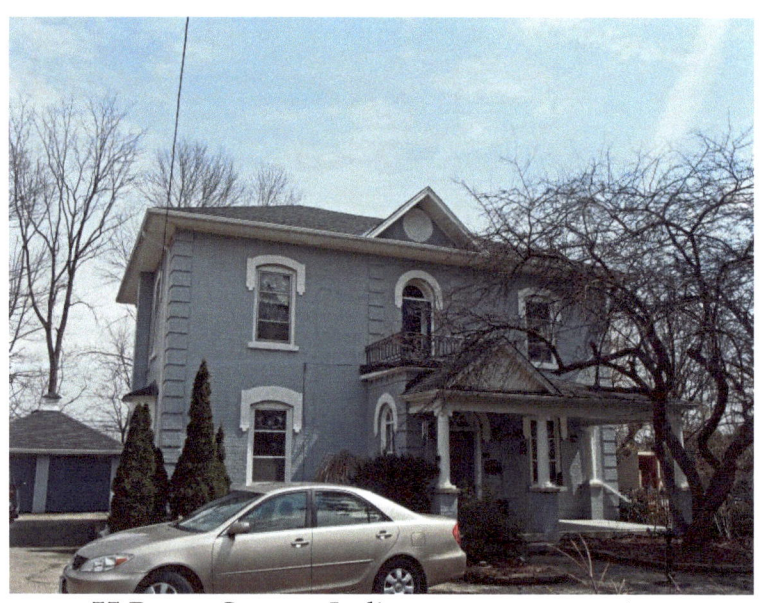

55 Byron Street – Italianate, corner quoins,
pediment above porch

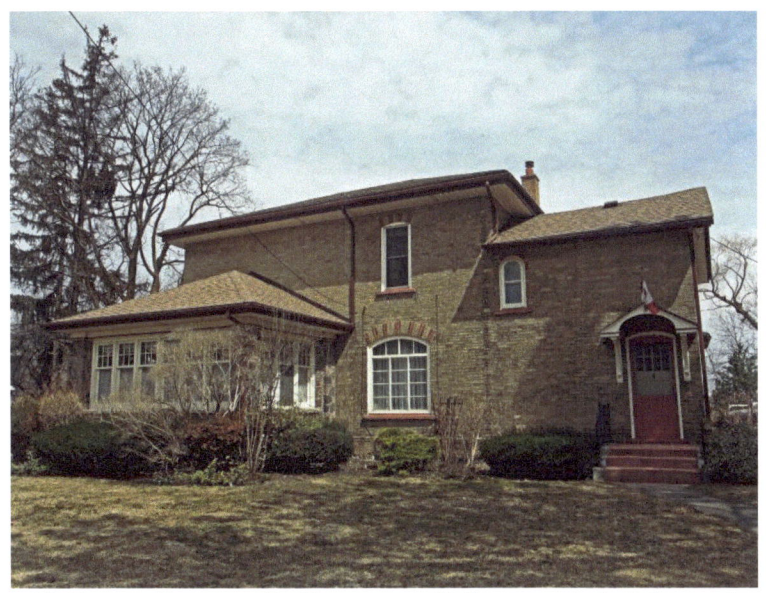

43 Byron Street – Italianate – dichromatic brickwork

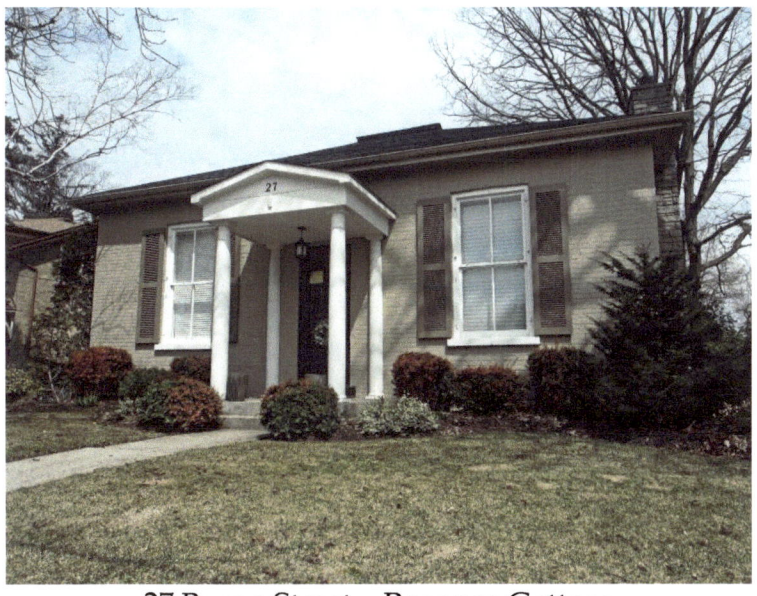

27 Byron Street – Regency Cottage

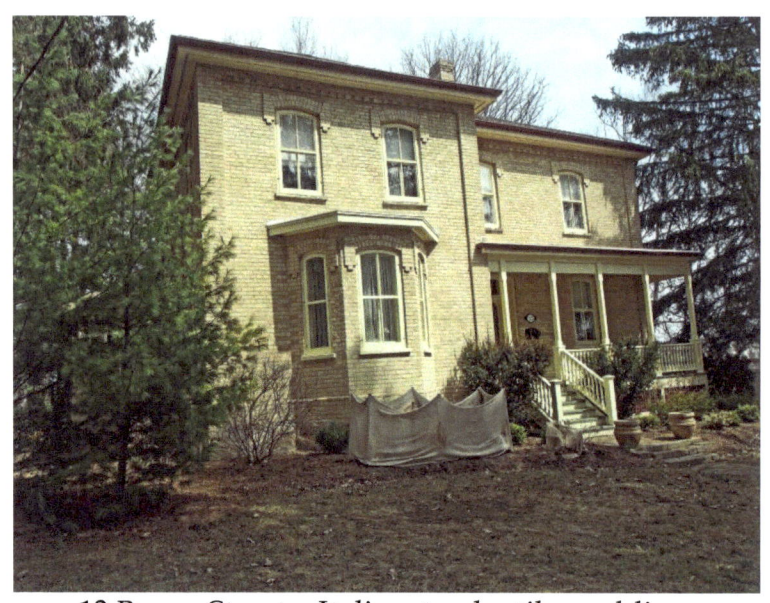

13 Byron Street – Italianate, dentil moulding, decorative window hoods

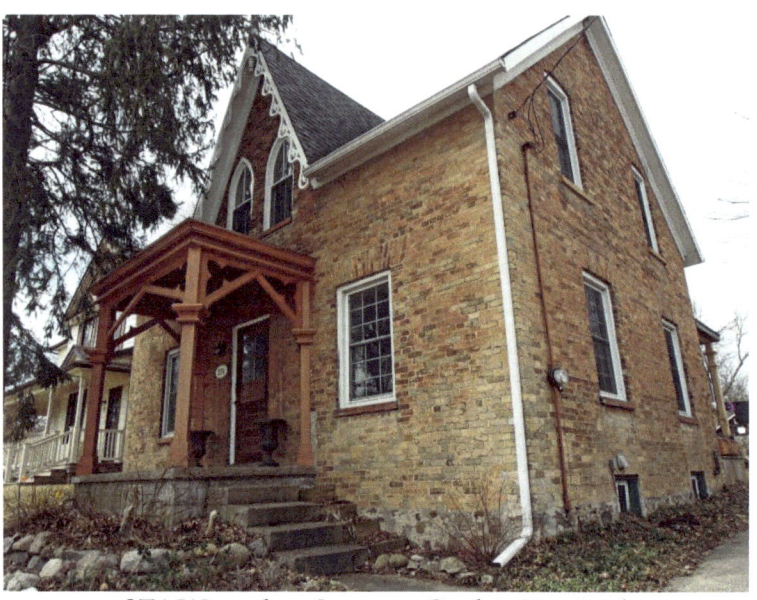

274 Waterloo Street – Gothic Revival

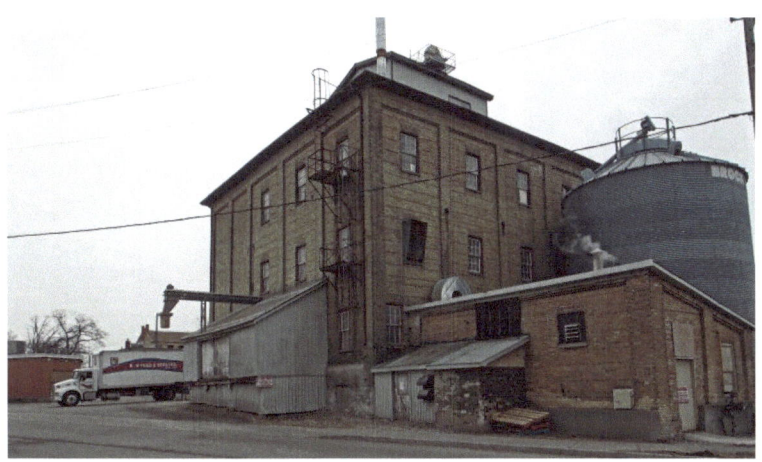

183 Mill Street – Flour Mill – built in 1905 after the three-storey frame mill building built in 1848 was destroyed by fire – water power was used for ten months of the year and steam for the other two months

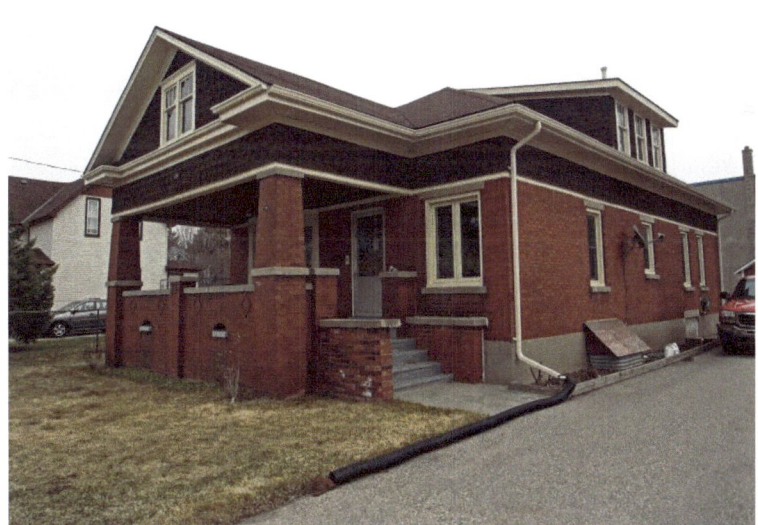

7 Seyler Drive – Italianate – dormer in roof, dormer with gable over the verandah

Architectural Terms

Bay Window: a window that projects out from a wall in a semicircular, rectangular, or polygonal design, used frequently in Gothic and Victorian designs. Example: 62 Byron Street	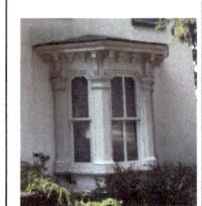
Belvedere: (from the Italian "beautiful view") an architectural feature on a roof, in a garden or on a terrace that gives a beautiful view. Example: 17 Huron Street	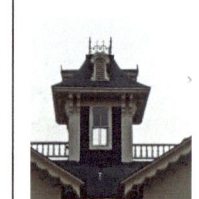
Brackets: a decorative or weight-bearing structural element which forms a right angle with one side against a wall and the other under a projecting surface such as an eave or roof. Example: 2 Byron Street	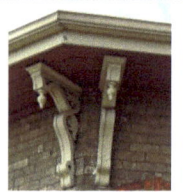
Buttress: a masonry structure built against or projecting from a wall which serves to support or reinforce the wall. In Canadian architecture, they are sometimes used for decoration. Example: 3 Byron Street	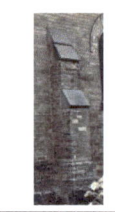
Cobblestone architecture: Refers to the use of cobblestones embedded in mortar as a method for erecting walls on houses and commercial buildings. Example: 166 Peel Street	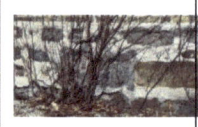

Cornice: originally the wooden overhang of the roof. With the use of stone, brick, iron and steel, the cornice is any projecting shelf at the top of a ceiling or roof. They can be very decorative. Example: 230 Peel Street	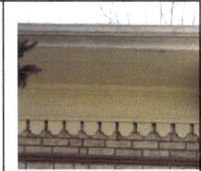
Cornice Return: decorative element on the end of a gable. Example: 120 Byron Street	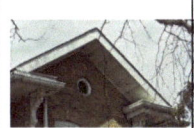
Decorative Window Hood: the horizontal architectural member in stone, wood or metal that spans an opening and supports the weight above it. Example: 349 Peel Street	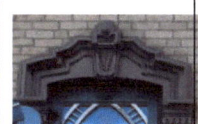
Dentil Moulding: an even series of rectangles used as ornamental decoration in cornices. Example: 349 Peel Street	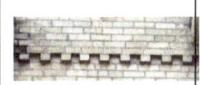
Dichromatic brickwork: the use of two colours of brick, tile or slate to decorate a façade. Example: 43 Byron Street	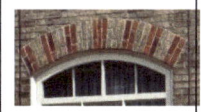
Dormer: (French for "sleep") a gable end window that pierces through the plane of a sloping roof surface to create usable space in the top floor or attic of a building by adding headroom. Example: 62 Byron Street	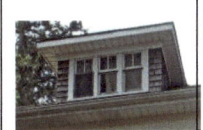
Finial: ornament added to the top of a gable, pinnacle, canopy or spire – a Gothic element. Example: 110 Byron Street	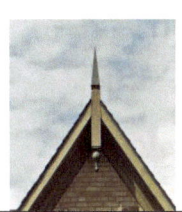

Fretwork: interlaced decorative design resembling a bracket Example: 96 Byron Street	
Gable: the triangular portion of a wall between the edges of a sloping roof. Example: 274 Waterloo Street	
Hipped Roof: a roof where all sides slope downwards to the walls with no gables. Example: 54 Byron Street	
Keystones and Voussoirs: a voussoir is a wedge-shaped element used in building an arch. A keystone is the central stone that locks all the stones into position, allowing the arch to bear weight. A keystone is often enlarged and embellished. This is a grape motif keystone. Example: 71-79 Huron Street	
Lancet Window: a tall, narrow window with a pointed arch at its top. Example: Zion United Church	
Palladian Window: a large window that is divided into three sections with the centre section larger than the two side sections and usually arched. Example: 258 Peel Street	

Pediment: a triangular section above the horizontal structure (entablature), typically supported by columns. The inside of the triangle is called the tympanum. Example: 55 Byron Street	
Pilaster: a slightly projecting column built into or applied to the face of a wall for additional structural support. Example: Huron Street	
Quoin: masonry blocks at the corner of a wall, often a decorative feature, usually larger or of a different colour than the rest of the wall. Example: 89 Byron Street	
Vergeboards: also called bargeboards – hang from the projecting end of a roof and are often elaborately carved and ornamented. Example: 244 Peel Street	

New Hamburg Building Styles

Beaux Arts: Promoters of this style sought to express the classical principles on a grand and imposing scale. Many of the Beaux Arts buildings were banks, post offices, and railway stations. The Ontario Beaux Arts style is eclectic mixing elements of Classical, Renaissance and Baroque. Often the designs have a temple-like façade, pedimented porticos, balustrades, capitals in many styles Example: New Hamburg Public Library	
Edwardian, 1900-1930 – This style bridges the ornate and elaborate styles of the Victorian era and the simplified styles of the 20th century. Balanced facades, simple roof lines, dormer windows, large front porches, and smooth brick surfaces are its characteristics. Example: 304 Peel Street	
Georgian, before 1860 – This style began with the British King Georges in the 18th century. These buildings have balanced facades around a central door, medium-pitched gable roofs, and small paned windows. Example: 257 Peel Street	
Gothic Revival, 1830-1890 – These decorative buildings have sharply-pitched gables with highly detailed vergeboards, pointed-arch window openings, and dichromatic brickwork. It is a common style in Ontario. Examples: 110 Byron Street, Black Walnut Cottage	